modern expressions

creating
fabulous and
fashionable
jewelry with
easy-to-find
elements

fernando dasilva

To my dear friend Katie, with a deepest admiration. Thanks for all your support. Beijos,

NORTH LIGHT BOOKS
CINCINNATI, OHIO

METRIC CONVERSION CHART

TO CONVERT	TO	MULTIPLY BY
inches	centimeters	2.54
centimeters	inches	0.4
feet	centimeters	30.5
centimeters	feet	0.03
yards	meters	0.9
meters	yards	1.1

www.fwmedia.com

14 13 12 11 10   5 4 3 2 1

DISTRIBUTED IN CANADA BY FRASER DIRECT
100 Armstrong Avenue
Georgetown, ON, Canada L7G 5S4
Tel: (905) 877-4411

DISTRIBUTED IN THE U.K. AND EUROPE BY F+W INTERNATIONAL
Brunel House, Newton Abbot, Devon, TQ12 4PU, England
Tel: (+44) 1626 323200, Fax: (+44) 1626 323319
E-mail: postmaster@davidandcharles.co.uk

DISTRIBUTED IN AUSTRALIA BY CAPRICORN LINK
P.O. Box 704, S. Windsor NSW, 2756 Australia
Tel: (02) 4577-3555

Library of Congress Cataloging-in-Publication Data
Dasilva, Fernando.
  Modern expressions / Fernando Dasilva.
    p. cm.
  Includes bibliographical references and index.
  ISBN-13: 978-1-4403-0672-3 (pbk. : alk. paper)
  ISBN-10: 1-4403-0672-9 (pbk. : alk. paper)
  1. Jewelry making. 2. Beadwork. 3. Wire jewelry. I. Title.
  TT212.D364 2010
  739.27--dc22
            2010024051

Editor: Rachel Scheller
Designer: Julie Barnett
Production Coordinator: Greg Nock
Photographer: Christine Polomsky
Stylist: Lauren Emmerling
Illustrator: Vladimir Alvarez

ABOUT THE AUTHOR

Fernando Dasilva was born and raised in Brasilia, the capital city of Brazil, and now resides in Pennsylvania, where he designs one-of-a-kind jewelry with a unique, cosmopolitan flair. The passion and beauty of Brazilian culture merges with European influences, the excitement of New York City and Fernando's world travels to create his vibrant, signature style.

Fernando says, "My jewelry is meant to make people feel glamorous and modern, even if they are just wearing jeans and a T-shirt."

Fernando's work has appeared in many beading magazines and in *Women's Wear Daily*, where he was noted as a designer to watch. He has appeared on the public television show *Beads, Baubles & Jewels* and has displayed jewelry in galleries and boutiques across the United States. He is the only male SWAROVSKI ELEMENTS brand ambassador and annually conducts workshops at the CREATE YOUR STYLE with SWAROVSKI ELEMENTS show in Tucson. He has created collections for Touchstone Crystal and Made by Me Jewelry and has been commissioned to create pieces for Beadalon, Swarovski and John Bead Corporation.

Fernando's jewelry collection is displayed at www.dasilvajewelry.com. He writes weekly posts about jewelry and lifestyle at www.modern-expressions.blogspot.com.

ACKNOWLEDGMENTS

I would like to thank the team at F+W Media, who put a precious amount of time, talent and vision into this book. Thank you to Christine Doyle, for embracing my ideas and giving me the opportunity to show my work to a wider audience. Thank you to Christine Polomsky, my photographer, and to Rachel Scheller, my editor, for supporting my ideas to create something unique. I also want to thank designer Julie Barnett, stylist Lauren Emmerling and production coordinator Greg Nock.

Many thanks to the companies that, through their products, enabled me to translate my inspirations into designs: Athenian Fashions, Artbeads.com, Beadalon, Elvee/Rosenberg, Great Craft Works, John Bead Corporation, Murano Glass Beads, Paula Radke Dichroics, Rio Grande, Star's Clasps and Swarovski North America through the CREATE YOUR STYLE division.

Thanks to Vlad Alvarez for the chic illustrations.

A special thanks to Kim Paquete, Katie Hacker and Margot Potter.

To my mother, Mirandulina, who gave me strength and courage and believed in my dreams.

My gratitude to Ascenate Leigh-Manuel, Alexandre Motta, Andrew Potter, Barb Switzer, Bruno Cardoso, Chuck Wolfmueller, Diane Murphy, Daniel John, Dawn Nials, Debbie Rosenberg, Deedee Ogilvie, Elizabeth Brehmer, Holly Haber, Jamie Hogsett, Janet Christy, John and Kae Goss, John Fritzinger, Leslie Rogalski, Lyn Kehoe, Mara Ortega, Matt Dubinsky, Mike Shields, Nadia Spano, Nicole Harper, Paula Radke, Rebecca Whittaker, Stan Paist, Stephan Toljan and Yvette Rodriguez.

Thanks to my beloved friends: Andre Luis Alves, Daniel and Terezinha Jr., Eliane Jacques, Fatima Carvalho, Aunt Jamin Alckmin, godmother Lindalva Gomes, Lucia Silva, Luis Lenza, Luigi Usai, Nilson and Vivily Quirino, Vera and Prasun Sinha, and the Trobilio Bastos family.

In memory of Cicero Lopes dos Santos, Janice Pingel, Jorge Gadioli, Luis A Caldas, Luis A. Jacques and Aunt Maria Magdalena.

Many soulful thanks to my guardian angel, Espoleta, Carrapicho, Jurema, Maria Conga, Ubirajara and Madame Ludeau. I feel your blessings every day of my life.

contents

introduction

Many years have passed since I strung my first beach wear necklace, but the passion for making something unique and original still drives my design inspirations. All of us struggle to keep our individuality intact so that we aren't just one more head in the middle of the crowd. In an effort to keep our identities in tune with our lifestyles, we make use of our natural talents to express our personalities, beliefs, cultural roots and deepest hopes. Jewelry-making is an activity that unleashes the spirit of imagination. It is a popular tool that people use to express their individuality. *Modern Expressions* brings some unexpected and vibrant additions to this creative, expressive artform.

Many people choose to represent their artistic visions through favorite colors, zodiac signs, lucky numbers and healing stones. My designs feature precious stones, wood, glass, acrylic and crystals to create your own contemporary and up-to-date jewelry box.

In the following pages, you will find an assortment of styles, colors and materials, as well as lots of information that will help you keep your identity in harmony with all the fun and unique looks that fill our world. This is your chance to have fun by making fashionable accessories and gather hints through fashion illustrations so you can get the most out of your new accessories. The "À La Mode" sketches are suggestions for how to wear the pieces, taking into consideration color, style and, in the case of the necklaces, the neckline. However, you may choose to wear your creations in new and different ways, and that's great too!

Eclectic and chameleonic, the designs in this book favor different personalities and offer many possibilities. As an extra feature, I have added a refined assortment of jewels in the Menswear Gallery (see page 116) to demonstrate how you can make something unique and cool for the guys as well.

The Resources section (see page 126) will provide you with the information you need to find the components in these designs. Keep in mind that the market releases new beads and new components often, and many times the hottest stone of today's season will be not available in the next one. If you can't find a particular component, flex your creative muscles and replace it with another finding. The addition may add a fresh perspective to the project.

Loosen your shoulders, take a deep breath and get ready to express your personality through 25 fabulous and fashionable designs. Welcome to the world of *Modern Expressions*.

materials

In my mind, jewelry and clothing are the only true artistic expressions for transforming ideas into body adornments. Rocks, paper, plastic, crystals, gemstones, feathers, glass, natural fibers, seeds, shells, terracotta, leather, leaves, metal, wood—all of these elements can be transformed into visual artistic expressions. There are several must-haves to achieve your desired look, some of which are listed here.

FINDINGS

Technically, findings refer to the fasteners and components used to assemble a piece of jewelry. They can be clasps, rings, eye and head pins, hooks, spacers, crimps, Bead Bumpers, ear wires, bails, connectors, caps, cones and cord ends, just to mention a few.

STRINGING MATERIAL

There are a wide range of stringing materials, from stainless steel wire and silk to rubber tubing and leather. This list can go on and on. I use stainless steel stringing wire for many of the projects in this book.

Beading wire is made from stranded threads of miniature stainless steel wire, making it as strong as steel but as soft as thread. The number of miniature wires determines its flexibility. You must choose the diameter that best fits the bead hole size, unless a specific wire is called for in the instructions.

Silk thread or cord is traditionally used to string pearls and other gemstones with a knot between each bead. It comes in a wide variety of colors and sizes, and you must pick the one that works best with the bead hole size. I normally use silk that is carded and comes with a needle already attached to it.

Velour and rubber tubing are sometimes hollow and can be used by themselves or sectioned and used as spacers between other components. They can also be combined with other stringing materials.

CHAIN

Any series of links connected together can be called chain. Chain is my favorite material to use when creating fashionable and trendy jewelry. It gives you a chance to be subtle or extravagant, romantic or tribal. Chain is one of the most versatile components in the jewelry-making world. In this book, I used chain made of wood, acrylic, base metal, precious metal and polyester. I also fashioned chain from jump rings and connectors.

BEADS

Incredible for their functionality and form, beads can be made of papier mâché, gemstones, acrylic, crystal, pearl, sponge, glass, ceramic and metal. Versatile and sometimes unexpected, beads can evoke glamour, romanticism, faith or nostalgia. As for gemstones, every season brings new stones into the jewelry market. With these additions comes a whole new spectrum of colors and shapes that excites designers all over the world and inspires them to create fresh pieces. Beads are an endless source of creativity, and I find it hard to imagine the existence of this book without them.

tools

It is unquestionable that good tools will always make better jewelry. In the jewelry market, where new gadgets are constantly released, it can be difficult to come up with a basic tool kit that will cover many different techniques. I considered the featured projects in this book and created a concise guide to help you differentiate the look and function of these tools.

PLIERS

Chain-nose pliers: Both jaws of these pliers are semi-round with flat surfaces where they meet. They can be used to open or close jump rings, close prongs and bead tips, and grip components and wire. I also use them to tuck excess wire under wrapped loops. I consider these the most versatile pliers.

Bent chain-nose pliers: The curved or bent tips of the jaws on these pliers allow you to grip your work with a larger "bite." When wire wrapping, the tips of the pliers won't be in your way.

Round-nose pliers: The jaws of these pliers are round and can be used to make eye pins, French wire earrings, clasps and jump rings. They are a must-have for forming and shaping wire.

Flat-nose pliers: These pliers have flat jaws and provide a wide area for gripping sheet metal, wire and components. They can also be used to create angled bends in metal. Two pairs of flat-nose pliers are very helpful when opening and closing jump rings.

Crimp pliers: These pliers are used to close crimp tubes or beads around stringing wire without compromising their strength and longevity. There are three sizes: micro, standard and mighty.

Nylon jaw pliers: These pliers protect the surface finish of wire and other materials. They are designed for shaping and sculpting Artistic Wire.

CUTTING TOOLS

Flush cutters: The jaws on flush cutters are designed to make a flush cut when using one side (usually the shiny side) and a pinch cut when using the other. Use the flush cut side when making your jewelry, as the pinch cut side will be very sharp. Flush cutters can be used with stringing wire, precious and nonprecious wires, and copper wire such as Artistic Wire.

Metal shears: These cutters have narrow blades that cut sheet metal. They are made of drop-forged steel and are heat-treated and tempered. In this book, I use them to cut copper sheet.

OTHER TOOLS

Beadalon Knotter Tool: This tool is used to make tight, consistent and professional-looking knotted strands of pearls. It can also be used with crystals and gemstones.

Bead opener tool: This is used to open a round, seamless metal bead. The pointed, long portion of the tool is called an awl.

Sbeady Wire Needle: This is a sharp, hollow needle with an easy-slide, half-open portion at the end for slipping the stringing wire into the hole. The needle can pierce velour, rubber tubing and other flexible materials.

Jump ring opener: This tool easily opens and closes jump rings. Slip it on your finger and use the slots in the tool to twist the rings.

Hole puncher: These pliers contain a pin on one side and a corresponding hole on the other side. They can be used on sheet metal to make a precise hole without rough edges.

precious

My fascination with colored gemstones prompted me to begin my first experiments in the jewelry design business. In the beginning, my eyes were hypnotized by the gleam of Brazilian gemstones. My first bestselling item was a necklace that alternated aquamarine rondelles and faceted peacock freshwater pearls, strung and knotted with turquoise silk thread. This piece became a staple on my design table, and the pearl-and-aquamarine duet remains a timeless ensemble. Every time I create a design using colored gemstones, I take into consideration not only the salability, but also the longevity of the design itself.

In this chapter, you will learn how to create pieces using some of the most popular colored gemstones. Taking a page from the ancient Greeks, I designed a double-stranded necklace

with 14-karat gold-filled wire, faceted pink quartz beads and subtle opalescent rondelles—a truly pink-and-gold *Extravaganza* (see page 12). In *Hip to be Square* (see page 16), I combined the gemstones with a fabric chain that adds a unique texture to the design and brings the shades of iolite, labradorite and onyx together. In *Chocolate Mint* (see page 20), a chocolate-colored chain is linked with sections of tiny peridot briolettes and smoky quartz beads and sustains two dramatic, fancy-cut green quartz drops.

All of these designs are incredibly wearable. The fashion sketches that accompany some of the designs are a guide to help you select the best outfits from your closet and set the right mood for your inner diva.

extravaganza

The Greeks were the first to alternate gold with colored gemstones, bringing a sense of high fashion into jewelry for the first time. I like the opulence of gold, and any gemstone looks fabulous once combined with it. In this design, excess meets uniqueness with modern fuchsia quartz and intricate pearl tablets.

This piece is delicately built on a repetition of beaded links connected together and spaced by an opalescent touch of crystals, creating a luxurious vibe.

MATERIALS

- 6' (1.8m) 24-gauge nontarnish half-hard brass wire
- eighteen 12mm × 9mm faceted fuchsia quartz cylinder beads
- thirty 16mm × 7.5mm top/side drilled mauve/champagne freshwater pearl tablets
- twenty-seven Swarovski Elements 8mm cyclamen opal briolette beads *Article 5040*
- six 8mm brushed vermeil spacer discs
- six 13mm × 10mm brushed vermeil flat oval spacer beads
- twelve 24mm × 8mm brushed vermeil two-hole marquis connectors
- forty-two 6mm gold-filled jump rings
- one 41mm textured vermeil toggle clasp

TOOLS

- chain-nose pliers
- flush cutters
- round-nose pliers

variation *Use six pearl tablets and two 20mm fuchsia quartz faceted coins. Assemble the earrings using the wrapping skills employed in the necklace. The oversized round pendants will get you lots of compliments, and people won't be able to take their eyes off you!*

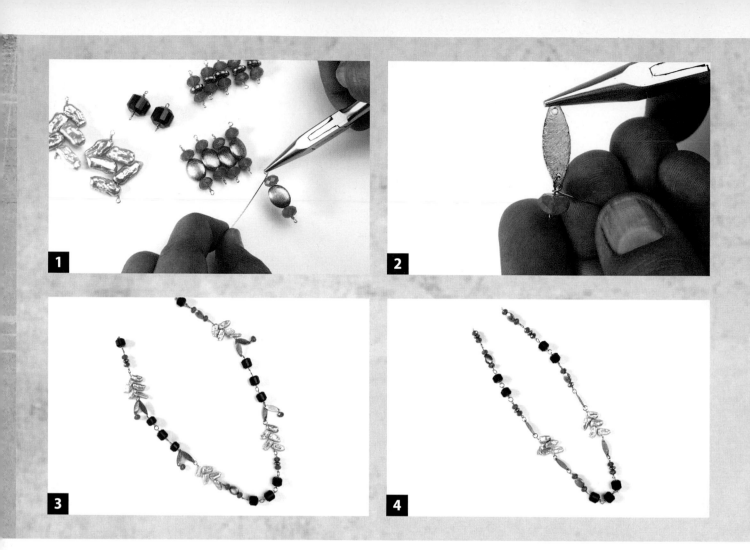

1 Make all components using nontarnish brass wire. Make a wrapped loop, string on the component and then make the same wrapped loop on the other side. For components with more than 1 bead, string on all components before making the 2nd wrapped loop. Create the following:
- 18 components with 1 fuchsia quartz bead (A)
- 6 components with 5 pearl tablets each (B)
- 5 components with cyclamen opal + vermeil spacer disc + cyclamen opal (C)
- 6 components with cyclamen opal + vermeil flat oval + cyclamen opal (D)

2 Cut 4 pieces of piece of brass wire, each measuring 2" (5.1cm). Use the tip of the round-nose pliers to fold down the tip of 1 of the wire ends. String on a cyclamen opal, make a half loop, slide on a marquis connector and complete the wrapped loop (E).

Note: When the pattern calls for a marquis dangle, slide the dangle and the next component in the pattern onto the next jump ring in the pattern.

3 Connect the components in the following pattern to make the longer strand of the necklace: jump ring + A + jump ring + C + jump ring + B + jump ring + D + E + marquis connector + jump ring + A + jump ring + A + jump ring + A + jump ring + E + marquis connector + jump ring + B + jump ring + D + jump ring + A + jump ring + A + jump ring + A + jump ring + C + jump ring + B + jump ring + marquis connector + jump ring + E + A + jump ring + A + jump ring + A + jump ring + marquis connector + jump ring + E + B + jump ring + D + jump ring + A + jump ring.

4 Connect components in the following pattern to make the shorter strand of the necklace: C + jump ring + D + jump ring + A + jump ring + A + jump ring + C + jump ring + marquis connector + jump ring + B + jump ring + marquis connector + jump ring + D + A + jump ring + A + jump ring + A + C + jump ring + marquis connector + jump ring + B + jump ring + marquis connector + jump ring + D + jump ring + A + jump ring + A + jump ring + C + jump ring + D.

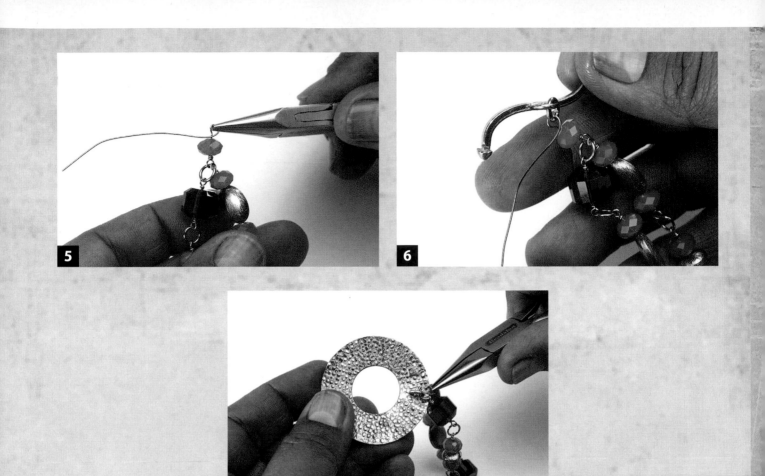

5 Cut a 2" (5.1cm) piece of wire and make a half loop at 1 end using round-nose pliers. Slide 1 end from the strands made in Steps 3 and 4 onto this loop. Finish making a wrapped loop and trim the excess wire. Slide a cyclamen opal bead onto the other end of the wire. Make a half loop on the other side of the bead.

6 Slide the toggle bar onto the half loop. Finish making a wrapped loop and trim the excess wire.

7 At the other end of the necklace, attach the strands together with a 6mm jump ring. Attach the toggle ring to the same jump ring and close it.

designer tip

Looking for guidance on opening and closing jump rings, making wrapped loops or using a crimp tube? Check out the Techniques section starting on page 118 for helpful step-by-step instructions.

SOURCES Beadalon, Rocky Mountain Gems & Minerals, Swarovski Elements

hip to be square

A combination of textures, form and iridescence, *Hip to be Square* is an architectural design that spotlights a matte black onyx square donut held in place by modern metal bails and frames. This project features a unique approach to mixing simple elements, transforming it into an art gallery accessory.

MATERIALS

- two sterling silver grooved donut bails
- one 30mm matte black onyx square donut
- two 3.5mm sterling silver oval Scrimp® Findings
- 12" (30.5cm) 19-strand .015" silver-plated stringing wire
- two sterling silver Wire Guardians™
- thirty-eight 6mm sterling silver jump rings
- sixteen 2mm satin silver oval Bead Bumpers™
- twenty-five 6mm faceted labradorite wide flat tire beads
- eight 7mm fire-polished black onyx round beads
- twelve 4mm iolite smooth round beads
- two sterling silver flared square bead frames
- 16" (40.6cm) gray polyester chain
- one sterling silver square knot toggle clasp

TOOLS

- chain-nose pliers
- flush cutters
- Scrimp® Findings screwdriver

à la mode *Choose a solid short-sleeve blouse with dark or metallic trim and a wide, square neckline that mimics the pendant's shape. Keep it demure and chic for the office and add a shawl or a jacket to attend a happy hour or an art exhibition after work.*

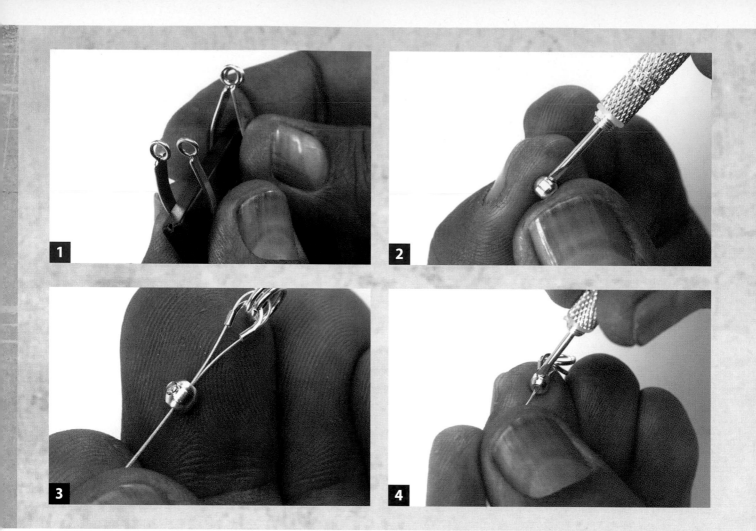

1 Attach 2 grooved donut bails around the black onyx donut. Open the bails carefully so they aren't pulled out of shape. Close the bails and set aside.

2 Loosen the screw of an oval Scrimp Finding and thread a 12" (30.5cm) piece of silver wire through it.

3 Feed the stringing wire onto a Wire Guardian, attach 2 jump rings and then thread the wire back through the Scrimp Finding.

4 Tighten the screw for a secure finish and trim the excess wire.

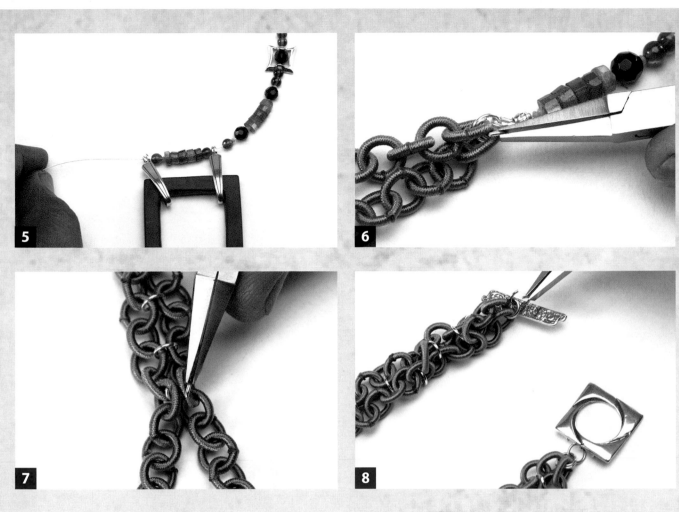

5 Start stringing beads as follows: 1 Bead Bumper + 5 labradorites + 1 Bead Bumper + 1 onyx + 2 iolites + 1 Bead Bumper + 1 bead frame with 1 onyx nested inside + 1 Bead Bumper + 2 iolites + 1 onyx + 1 Bead Bumper + 5 labradorites + 1 Bead Bumper + 1 onyx + 1 Bead Bumper + 1 iolite.

String on the pendant assembled in Step 1, threading the wire through the rings of the 1st bail and then stringing 1 iolite + 1 Bead Bumper + 5 labradorites + 1 Bead Bumper + 1 iolite. Thread the wire through the rings of the 2nd bail.

Repeat the pattern in Step 5 in reverse order to finish the beaded portion of the necklace symmetrically. Add a Scrimp Finding, Wire Guardian and 2 jump rings to the end of the beaded portion as described in Steps 2–4.

6 Cut 16" (40.6cm) of polyester chain into 4 equal sections. Attach a piece of chain to the jump rings on each end of the beaded portion of the necklace piece. Add 2 more jump rings to each opposite side of the polyester chain ends.

7 Link the remaining 2 strands of polyester chain to the strands on the necklace by connecting every other link with silver-plated jump rings.

8 Using a single jump ring on each end, add a toggle ring and bar to the ends of the necklace.

SOURCES Beadalon, John Bead Corporation

chocolate mint

Applying ordinary elements to create original pieces can be challenging, but when innovation meets classic, anything can be reinvented, even a lariat necklace. This color palette might seem safe at first glance, but vibrant green quartz makes it updated. An eccentric chocolate-colored sterling silver chain serves as a perfect background for vivid peridot and sensual smoky topaz. Two modern green quartz briolettes illuminate the neckline, making this design the perfect accessory for the red carpet. Strike a pose!

MATERIALS

- 4' (1.2m) 24-gauge nontarnish round half-hard wire

- two 24mm × 18mm tourma-line green quartz fancy-cut triangle drops

- five 13.5mm × 7mm center-drilled smoky topaz teardrop beads

- 24" (61cm) chocolate-colored sterling silver cable chain

- thirteen 8.5mm × 5mm peridot briolettes

- two 6mm 20-gauge gold-filled jump rings

- one 41mm brushed vermeil G toggle clasp

TOOLS

- chain-nose pliers

- flush cutters

- round-nose pliers

1 Cut a 3" (7.6cm) piece of nontarnish wire and string on a tourmaline triangle stone, positioning it ½" (1.3cm) from the end. Carefully bend both ends of the wire straight up. Wrap the shorter wire around the longer wire 2 full revolutions. Cut the excess wire from the shorter wire. Use round-nose pliers to make a wrapped loop with the longer wire.

2 Cut a 3" (7.6cm) piece of nontarnish wire and make a half loop at the end. Connect this loop to the tourmaline triangle from Step 1 and then complete the wrapped loop. Trim the excess wire. Add a smoky topaz bead to the wire and then form a matching loop on the opposite end, but do not close it. Repeat Steps 1 and 2 and set these components aside.

3 Cut a 12" (30.5cm) piece of chain. Fold the chain in half and tie a knot so there is a loop at the top and 2 loose ends at the bottom.

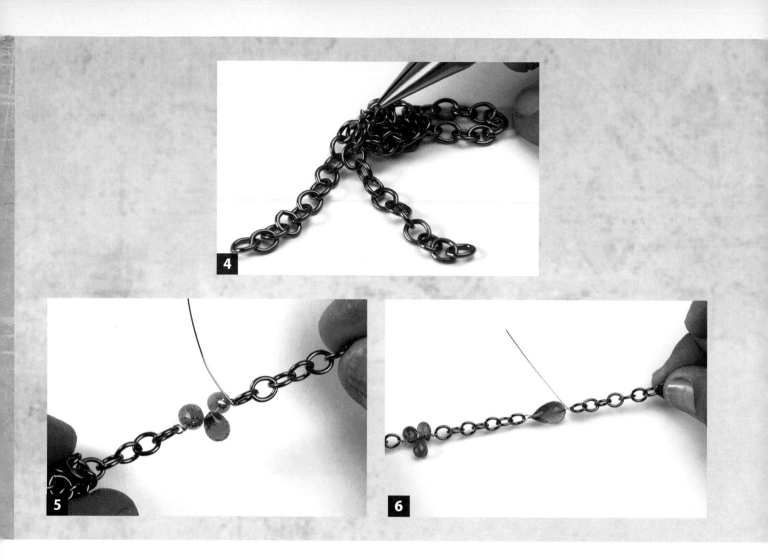

4 Cut several links of a separate piece of chain to
serve as jump rings. Slip these jump rings into the
knotted part of the chain and close them to secure
the knot in several places. Snip the loop above the
knot in half. The resulting ends will begin the 2
halves of the necklace.

5 Make a half loop with 3" (7.6cm) of nontarnish wire
and connect it with 1 of the chain ends above the
knot. Slide on 3 peridot briolettes and nest them.
Make another half loop at the other end of the
briolettes and slide on a 1¼" (3.2cm) piece of chain.
Complete the wrapped loops on both sides of the
briolettes and trim the excess wire.

6 Repeat Step 5 using a smoky topaz briolette and a
1¼" (3.2cm) piece of chain.

designer tip

When cutting chain to make jump rings,
always cut on the soldered part of the
link. This removes the rough area of the
solder and allows the ring to be opened
and closed without much fatigue.

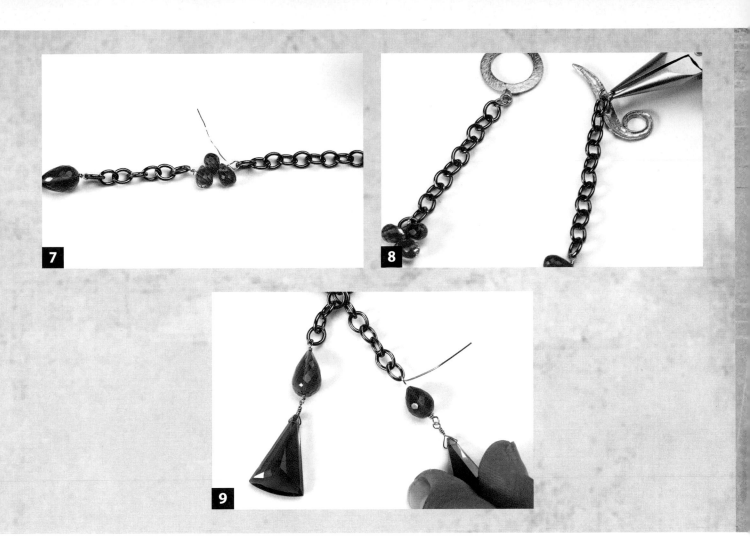

7 Repeat Step 5 using 3 peridot briolettes and a 2¼"
(5.7cm) piece of chain.

8 Repeat Steps 5–7 to complete the other half of the
necklace. Once both halves are complete, attach
the toggle ring and bar to the ends of the necklace
with 2 6mm gold-filled jump rings.

9 Slide the unclosed loops of the components from
Steps 1–2 to the bottom chains of the necklace.
Complete the loops by wrapping the excess wire
2 full revolutions around the base of the loop and
then cut the excess wire.

SOURCES Beadalon, Rio Grande, Rocky Mountain Gems
& Minerals, Star's Clasps

night and day duet

Gabrielle Coco Chanel was the first designer to incorporate ropes of beads into fashion philosophy, and she became a legend after accessorizing a black pullover with several strands of pearls. I created this ensemble with two fashion staples in mind: Chanel beaded long necklaces and the classic look of black and white.

I created a short wavy necklace to be worn with a longer black strand in a similar color palette. The simplicity of the lines in both pieces will take your ensemble directly to understated elegance.

MATERIALS

SHORT NECKLACE

- two #3 sterling silver crimp tubes
- 22" (55.9cm) 19-strand .024" silver-plated bright stringing wire
- two large sterling silver Wire Guardians™
- 1 sterling silver marquis-shaped toggle clasp
- twenty-two sterling silver curved spacer tubes
- four 8mm black/gold/silver round Venetian glass beads
- ten 10mm black onyx soccer ball cut round beads
- three 12mm silver/gold foil abacus Venetian glass beads
- four 15mm white coral round beads

LONG NECKLACE

- 12" (30.5cm) 20-gauge silver-plated German style wire
- four 5mm × 2.65mm sterling silver smooth rondelles

- one 35mm black line agate coin bead
- one 30mm silver/gold foil Venetian glass coin bead
- one card of #12 black silk
- two sterling silver cup bead tips
- thirty-seven 10mm black onyx soccer ball cut round beads
- nine 12mm black onyx soccer ball cut round beads
- ten 6mm × 3.3mm sterling silver smooth rondelles
- eight 6mm gold-filled saucer beads
- seven 14mm faceted white howlite round beads
- two sterling silver marquis-shaped beads
- three Swarovski Elements 16mm jet chessboard beads *Article 5005*
- one sterling silver white mother-of-pearl mosaic toggle clasp

TOOLS

- Beadalon Bead Stringing Glue
- Beadalon Knotter Tool
- chain-nose pliers
- flush cutters
- round-nose pliers

à la mode *The classic and dressy style of the necklaces creates an opportunity for you to wear one of the most dramatic trends in fashion: black and white. You can go with a classic black suit and white shirt, but a white suit keeps things soft and sophisticated. Carry accessories in any color, or keep it low key by bringing out the gold accents in the necklaces with a gold clutch. A hint of a men's tailoring doesn't hurt!*

SHORT NECKLACE

1 String a #3 crimp tube onto 1 end of a 22" (55.9cm) piece of 19-strand beading wire. String on a large Wire Guardian and the toggle bar. Thread the wire back through the crimp tube and crimp.

2 String on beads as follows: curved spacer + black/gold/silver Venetian + curved spacer + onyx + curved spacer + silver/gold Venetian + curved spacer + onyx + curved spacer + coral round + onyx + curved spacer + black/gold/silver Venetian + curved spacer + onyx + curved spacer + coral round + curved spacer + onyx + curved spacer + silver/gold Venetian + curved spacer + onyx + curved spacer + coral round + curved spacer + onyx + curved spacer + black/gold/silver Venetian + curved spacer + onyx + curved spacer + coral round + curved spacer + onyx + curved spacer + silver/gold Venetian + curved spacer + onyx + curved spacer + black/gold/silver Venetian + curved spacer.

3 Attach the toggle ring to the other end of the necklace following the same process as in Step 1.

SOURCES Beadalon, Murano Glass Beads, Rio Grande

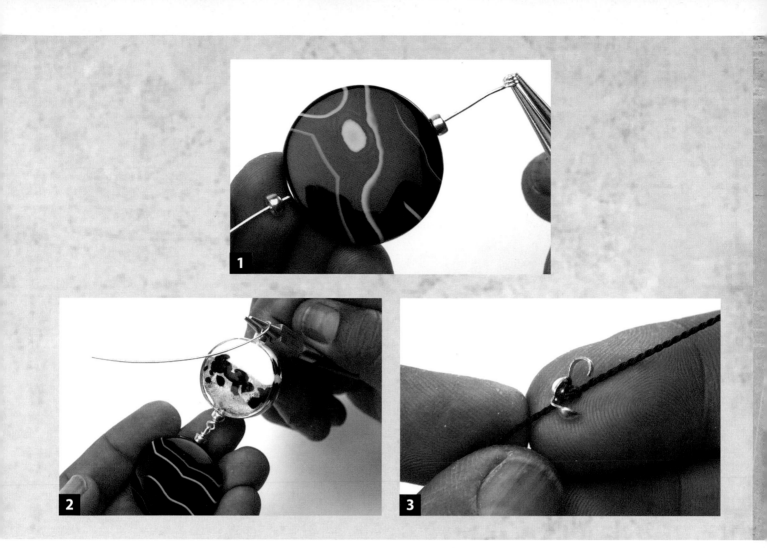

LONG NECKLACE

1 Cut 2 pieces of German style wire measuring 6"
(15.2cm). Create a corkscrew swirl at the end of 1
piece of wire by wrapping the wire 3 times around
the tip on the round-nose pliers. String on beads
as follows: 5mm rondelle + black line agate coin +
5mm rondelle. Make a wrapped loop after the last
rondelle and trim the wire.

2 Make a half loop at the end of the other 6" (15.2cm)
piece of wire. Attach this loop to the component
from Step 1, then complete the loop with 2
wraps. String on beads as follows: 5mm rondelle +
Venetian glass coin + 5mm rondelle. Set this piece
aside; you will finish the end later when you attach
it to the necklace.

3 Unroll a card of #12 black silk, pulling firmly so that
all of the kinks come out and the silk feels a little
stiff. Tie a knot at the end of the silk and string on a
cup bead tip.

designer tip

Many people believe that pulling silk
firmly will stretch it out of shape, but
doing this simply pulls the twist tighter
so the knots will stay tight.

4 Begin stringing beads as follows: 2 10mm onyx + 12mm onyx + 2 10mm onyx + 6mm rondelle + howlite + 6mm rondelle + 2 10mm onyx + 12mm onyx + 2 10mm onyx + gold-filled saucer + howlite + gold-filled saucer + 2 10mm onyx + 12mm onyx + 2 10mm onyx + 6mm rondelle + howlite + 6mm rondelle + 2 10mm onyx + 12mm onyx + 2 10mm onyx + gold-filled saucer + howlite + gold-filled saucer + 2 10mm onyx + 12mm onyx + 2 10mm onyx + gold-filled saucer + howlite + gold-filled saucer + 2 marquis-shaped + 2 10mm onyx + 12mm onyx + 2 10mm onyx + gold-filled saucer + howlite + gold-filled saucer + 10mm onyx + 6mm rondelle + chessboard + 6mm rondelle + chessboard + 6mm rondelle + chessboard + 6mm rondelle + 2 10mm onyx + 12mm onyx + 2 10mm onyx + gold-filled saucer + howlite + gold-filled saucer + 2 10mm onyx + 12mm onyx + 2 10mm onyx + 6mm rondelle + howlite + 6mm rondelle + 2 10mm onyx + 12mm onyx + 2 10mm onyx.

5 Starting at the end of the necklace with the cup bead tip, begin knotting using a knotter tool. Place a knot between each onyx bead. In sequences of [rondelle + howlite + rondelle] or [saucer + howlite + saucer], place a knot before the 1st rondelle or saucer and after the 2nd rondelle or saucer. At the center of the necklace, between the marquis-shaped beads, tie 2 knots next to each other. Continue knotting to the other end of the necklace.

6 Thread the silk through a cup bead tip and cut the silk, leaving 3" (7.6cm) of excess. Divide the excess silk in half and tie a double knot tightly on the inside of the cup.

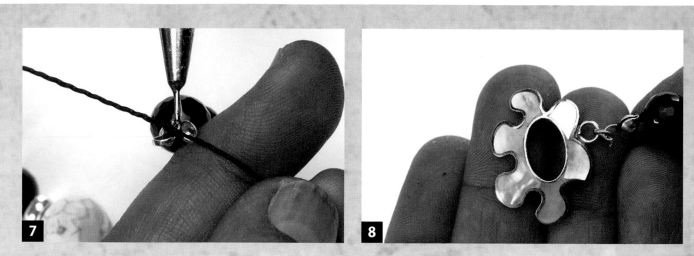

7 Glue the knots on both bead tips with bead stringing glue. Let the glue dry before cutting the excess silk.

8 Attach the toggle ring to the cup bead tip loop on 1 side and the toggle bar to the loop on the other side. Use chain-nose pliers to close the bead tips.

9 Form a half loop with the wire from the component from Steps 1–2 and attach it between the 2 knots at the center of the necklace. Wrap the excess wire around the base of the loop 2 full revolutions. Cut the excess wire.

designer tip

It is best to let the glue dry for 24 hours before cutting the excess silk.

SOURCES Beadalon, Murano Glass Beads, Star's Clasps

deco chic

The showcases of this project are the modern sterling silver diamond-shaped connectors. I believe that when findings are extraordinarily pretty, you don't need to add much to them. I could have wrapped two rows of little stones to the connectors, but so many stones would have covered most of the polished surface. Flawless emerald-cut citrine pendants illuminate these earrings, while amethyst pendants and black spinnel briolettes add depth to the architectural silhouette.

MATERIALS

- 24" (61cm) 26-gauge sterling silver round half-hard wire

- eight 8mm × 6mm top-drilled amethyst emerald-cut pendants

- four 10mm × 7.5mm top-drilled citrine emerald-cut pendants

- two 30mm sterling silver 3-diamond pendants

- two 16mm × 14mm × 2mm black spinnel fancy-cut triangle briolettes

- two 6mm sterling silver jump rings

- two 4mm sterling silver jump rings

- one pair of polished modern square ear posts

TOOLS

- bent chain-nose pliers

- flush cutters

- round-nose pliers

à la mode *A printed boho silk blouse is a fabulous choice to accentuate the retro cool style of these chandelier earrings. Big earrings are helpful in drawing the eye away from an ample bust.*

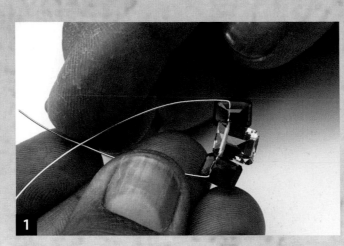

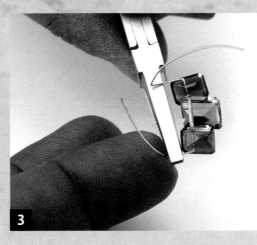

1 String the following beads onto a 4" (10.2cm) piece of 26-gauge sterling silver wire: amethyst with pavilion or back side facing forward + citrine with front facing forward + amethyst with pavilion side facing forward. Arrange the stones so they sit snugly together in the center of the wire. Bend each side of the wire straight up.

2 Carefully bend the wire on the right side of the component from Step 1 at a right angle approximately ¼" (6mm) above the hole in the amethyst stone. The wire should now be running toward the back of the component. Repeat this step on the left side.

3 Place the component inside the bottom right opening in a diamond pendant. The 2 wires should be inside the opening. Carefully bend the right-side wire down and over the pendant, then up and around, securing the component. Repeat this step on the left side.

designer tip

When working with new wire techniques, it's a good idea to practice wrapping the wire prior to working with the gemstones. Do not bend the wire too close to the hole in the gemstone, as this may cause it to fracture. Consider using clear Bead Bumpers on the ends where you have to bend the wire. These will provide some "give" so the hole in the gemstone doesn't have to.

4 Trim the right-side wire, leaving enough excess so it can be pushed through the opening again and bent flat against the diamond pendant (the wire should make 1½ revolutions around the pendant bar). Gently squeeze the end of the wire in the back with bent chain-nose pliers so the end doesn't stick out. Cut the excess wire. Repeat this on the left side.

Repeat Steps 1–4 on the opposite side of the diamond pendant.

5 Using a 3" (7.6cm) piece of sterling silver wire, string on a triangle spinnel drop. Bend both ends of the wire straight up and attach the drop to the bottom of the diamond pendant in the same manner as described in Steps 3–4 (the wire should make 1½ revolutions around the pendant bar). Adjust the wraps so the wires are pushed toward the V shape at the bottom of the pendant. Trim the excess wire.

6 Attach a 6mm jump ring to the top V shape of the diamond pendant. Attach a 4mm jump ring to the 6mm jump ring. Attach an earring post to the 4mm jump ring. Repeat Steps 1–6 for the other earring.

SOURCES Beadalon, Bijoux Collection, John Bead Corporation

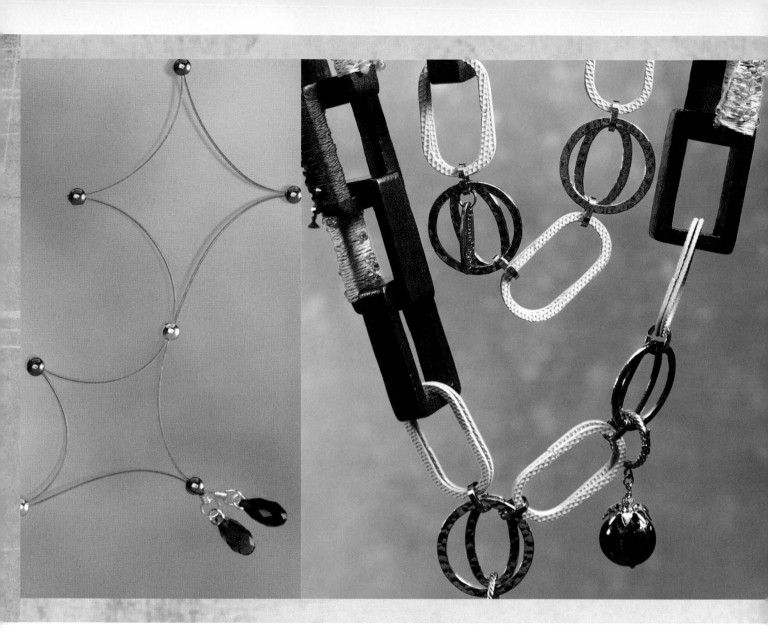

chain of command

Few components in the jewelry-making world provide more design versatility than chain. Technically, any material that has been linked together can be called a chain, and it's fair to say that from the moment humans started hunting, chains made of bones, teeth, claws and shells were strung on thread, fiber or leather and worn around the neck or the wrist.

Around 2500 B.C., the Egyptians started dynamically alternating beads with metals like copper and silver to create chains that were called jewelry for the first time. They had a great affection for chain necklaces and bracelets. This kind of jewelry was worn for many different reasons, from declaring religious beliefs to displaying social status.

Dimensional pendants and gold were introduced during the Classical Greek period, and by the second century, chains consisted of colored gemstones interlocked with gold links. These pieces introduced the idea of a high-fashion trend.

In the modern jewelry-making market, several chain styles are widely available, from plastic, wood and polyester to stone, brass and gold. You can even find beaded linked chains that are ready to be assembled.

CHAPTER 2

For the lovers of the Bohemian lifestyle, I mixed crystal cotton yarn with large links of wooden chain; *Square n' Yarn* (see page 36) pushes glamour to grand proportions. In *Fantasia* (see page 46), you will learn how easy it is to create a substantial treasure-style bracelet using heavy textured cable chain and bold glass pendants. I pair black-and-white Lucite links with crystal components in a *Dazzling Retro* design that evokes the Art Deco movement and its timeless elegance (see page 50). *Netted Choker* (see page 54) experiments with astonishing Beadalon SilveRose stringing wire to build a stretchy design that fits the neckline perfectly.

Considering that chain is the main structure for many jewelry pieces, you will find different styles of chain throughout this book that work as background support for other highlighted jewelry elements. I invite you to break the links that hold back your creativity and free your mind to experiment with these designs.

square n' yarn

This design combines globalization and eclecticism, a fusion of the South American laid-back attitude and European elegance. Large square links of wood are partially covered with beaded yarn and sectioned with colored oval links to celebrate the Bohemian style of life through casual comfort and earthy harmony. Adorned with interchangeable turquoise and Venetian glass dangles, this necklace will get you tons of compliments.

MATERIALS

- 24" (61cm) rectangle link wood chain
- 2 yds (1.8m) Swarovski Elements pink and vintage rose cotton yarn *Article 59000*
- 2 yds (1.8m) Swarovski Elements brown and crystal dorado cotton yarn *Article 59000*
- 2 yds (1.8m) Swarovski Elements blue and caribbean opal cotton yarn *Article 59000*
- fifteen 1.6mm gold-plated heavy oval rings
- twenty-two beige-colored brass oval chain links
- eight 27mm gold-plated textured solid round rings

- eight 17mm × 30mm gold-plated textured solid oval rings
- four gold-plated flower bead caps
- four 2" (5.1cm) gold-plated ball head pins
- two 25mm rose gold Venetian glass beads
- four 6mm gold-plated beaded rings
- four 4mm brushed gold-plated crimp covers
- four gold-plated enhancer bails
- two 15mm × 22mm faceted stabilized turquoise barrel beads

TOOLS

- Beadalon Bead Stringing Glue
- chain-nose pliers
- flush cutters
- Mighty Crimper Tool
- round-nose pliers

à la mode
Pairing this necklace with a tunic worn as a mini-dress, a roomy red leather bag and light brown strappy sandals exudes a carefree attitude without losing a bit of sophistication. Although the washed gray tunic takes you to a fall palette, the elements combined say summer time.

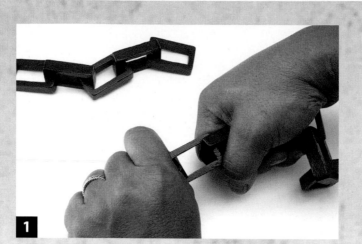

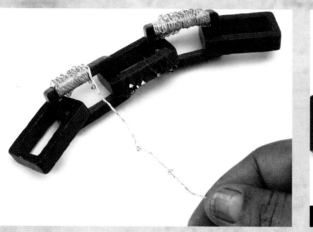

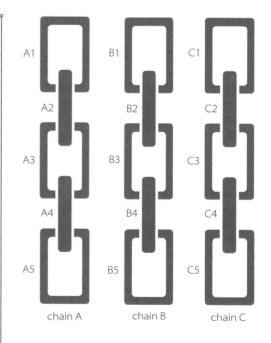

1 Break the wooden chain into 3 pieces of 5 links each (chains A, B and C). To break the chain easily, hold it in each hand and twist. Set the pieces aside. Each of these links will be referred to as A1, A2, A3, A4 and A5; B1, B2, B3, B4 and B5; and C1, C2, C3, C4 and C5 (see diagram at right).

2 With chain A, wrap 24" (61cm) of pink beaded yarn around link A2. Tie 2 simple knots at each end of the link to secure the yarn. Add a dab of bead stringing glue after the 2nd knot and trim the excess, leaving a small amount of fringe at the ends. Repeat this process on link A3 using brown beaded yarn, and on link A4 using pink beaded yarn.

3 With chain B, wrap 24" (61cm) of blue beaded yarn around link B2. Repeat the tying and gluing instructions from Step 2. Repeat this process on link B3 using brown beaded yarn, and on link B4 using pink beaded yarn.

A1   B1   C1

A2   B2   C2

A3   B3   C3

A4   B4   C4

A5   B5   C5

chain A   chain B   chain C

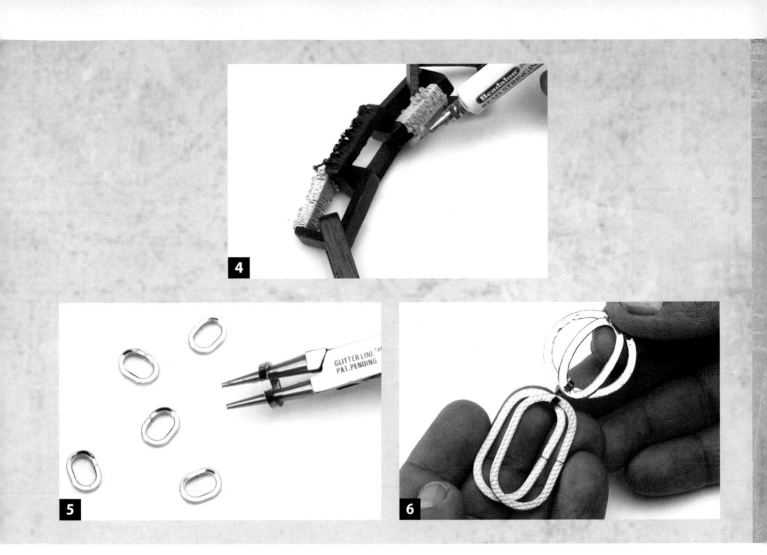

4 With chain C, wrap 24" (61cm) of blue beaded
   yarn around link C2. Repeat the tying and gluing
   instructions from Step 2. Repeat this process on
   link C3 using brown beaded yarn, and on link C4
   using blue beaded yarn.

5 Using round-nose pliers, open each gold-plated
   heavy oval ring by inserting both ends of the pliers
   inside a ring and carefully opening the pliers.

6 Separate the beige-colored chain links. Connect
   a pair of beige links to a pair of 1 round and 1 oval
   gold-plated textured rings with an opened heavy
   oval ring. Close the heavy oval ring with the Mighty
   Crimp Tool.

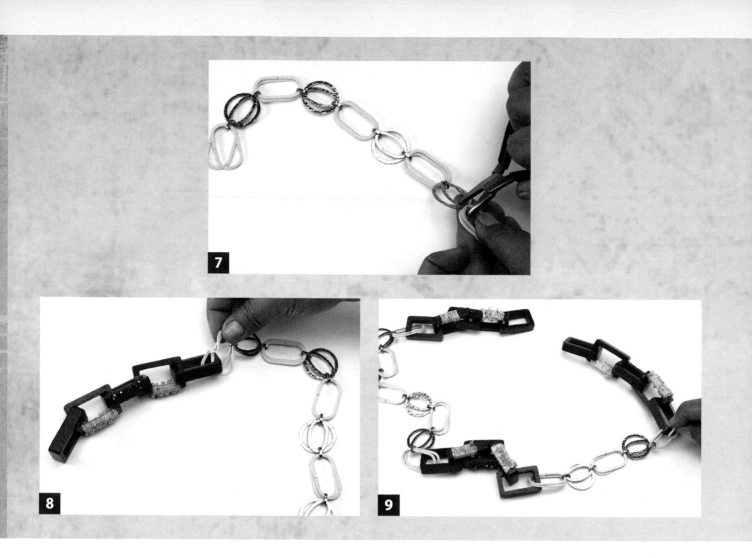

7 Connect the following to the pair of textured rings from Step 6: heavy oval ring + pair of beige links + heavy oval ring + pair of 1 round and 1 oval textured rings + heavy oval ring. Repeat this pattern 2 more times and then attach another pair of beige-colored links to the end.

8 Open the pair of beige links on each end of the chain made in Step 7 and attach 1 end to link A1 on wood chain A. Attach the other end of the metal chain to C5 on wood chain C.

9 Create a similar chain as the one from Steps 6–7, using the same pattern but stopping after the 3rd pair of beige links. Open the pair of beige links on both sides of this chain and attach 1 end to link A5 on wood chain A and the other end to link B1 on wood chain B.

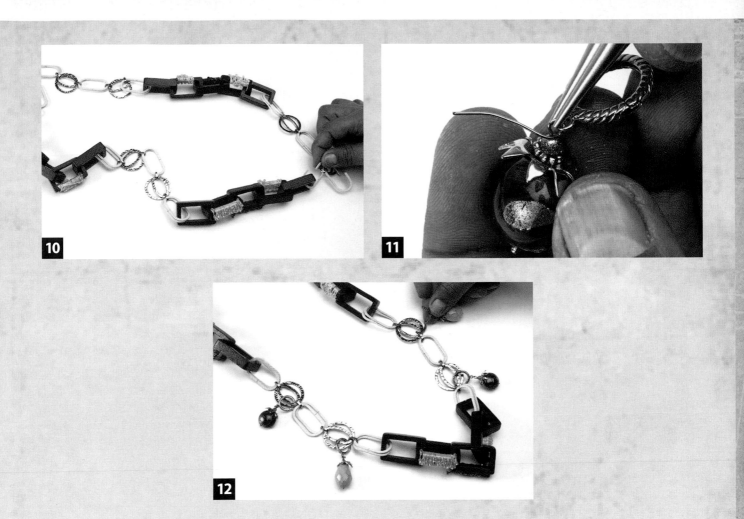

10 Repeat Step 9 to create a 3rd metal chain, stopping after the 3rd pair of beige links. Open the pair of beige links on both sides of this chain and attach 1 end to link B5 on wood chain B and the other end to link C1 on wood chain C.

11 Use chain-nose pliers to bend down all edges of the flower bead caps. String the following onto a ball head pin: Venetian bead + bead cap with "petals" covering bead + beaded ring + closed crimp cover. After the crimp cover, make a loop with the head pin, and then slide on a gold-plated enhancer bail. Wrap the excess wire around the base of the loop 2 full revolutions. Repeat this step 3 more times with the remaining Venetian bead and 2 turquoise beads.

12 Attach the beaded enhancer bails from Step 11 randomly to any of the metal or wooden links.

designer tip

Enhancer bails are great for controlling the amount of bling you want on your necklace. You can also attach enhancer bails to existing jewelry for added flair. They are great for jazzing up any jewelry item.

SOURCES Beadalon, Swarovski

velvet underground

Inspired by the lavish look of many Latin American women in my life, I created this exuberant design, structured with large circles of sparkling gunmetal chain. In this design I followed the principle that if the pattern is busy, the frame must be simple, yet sophisticated. Radiant purple and jet crystals are placed within some of the links and dangle in clusters from others. This necklace emulates Salma Hayek, Penelope Cruz, Sonia Braga and many other gorgeous Latin divas.

MATERIALS

- 30" (76.2cm) gunmetal etched large circle chain

- 6" (15.2cm) gunmetal medium square cable chain

- thirty-six 2" (5.1cm) gunmetal ball head pins

- eight Swarovski Elements 17mm × 9mm jet 2-hole keystone beads *Article 5181*

- twenty-eight black round Bead Bumpers™

- eighteen Swarovski Elements 10mm purple velvet Helix beads *Article 5020*

- eighteen Swarovski Elements 8mm tanzanite Xilion beads *Article 5328*

- three 14mm black brushed brass round beads

- nineteen 12mm black brass jump rings

- one 41mm gunmetal swivel badge clip

TOOLS

- chain-nose pliers

- flat chain-nose pliers

- flush cutters

- round-nose pliers

à la mode *Embrace your curves and try a voluptuous look, keeping in mind that when the design is busy, the frame needs to be simpler. An electric purple party dress with no beading will welcome any statement necklace. Here, a revealing cleavage line is toned down by the variety of geometric shapes in the necklace. Add matching earrings and sexy satin open-toe heels and release your inner diva.*

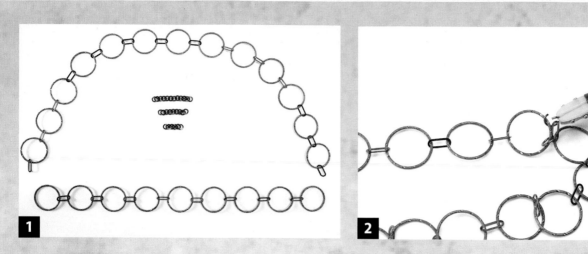

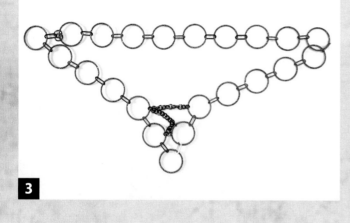

1 Cut a piece of large circle chain to 13 circles, leaving the oval links attached at each end. Cut another piece of large circle chain to 9 circles, omitting the oval links at the ends. Cut a piece of square cable chain to 27 links.

2 Connect the end of the 9-link large circle chain to the end of the 13-link large circle chain using 2 12mm jump rings. Connect the chains on the other side in the same manner.

3 Arrange the necklace so the 2 ends of the 9-link large circle chain and the center link of the 13-link large circle chain form the points of a triangle. Connect the end of the 27-link square cable chain to the circle to the left of the center circle on the 13-link large circle chain. Connect the 7th link on the cable chain to the circle to the right of the center circle. Connect the 17th link on the cable chain 2 links to the left of the center circle. Connect the other end of the cable chain to the circle 2 links to the right of the center circle. The resulting zigzag pattern will hold the center of the necklace together so it will sit correctly on the neck.

4 Make keystone links by feeding a ball head pin through a hole in a keystone bead. String on the following: Bead Bumper + purple velvet bead + Bead Bumper. Make a simple loop large enough to attach to the large circle chain. Trim the excess wire.

Thread a ball head pin through the other hole in the keystone bead, going the opposite direction from the 1st head pin. String on the following: Bead Bumper + purple velvet bead + Bead Bumper. Make a large simple loop to match the 1st simple loop. Trim the excess wire. Repeat this step to make 6 more keystone links.

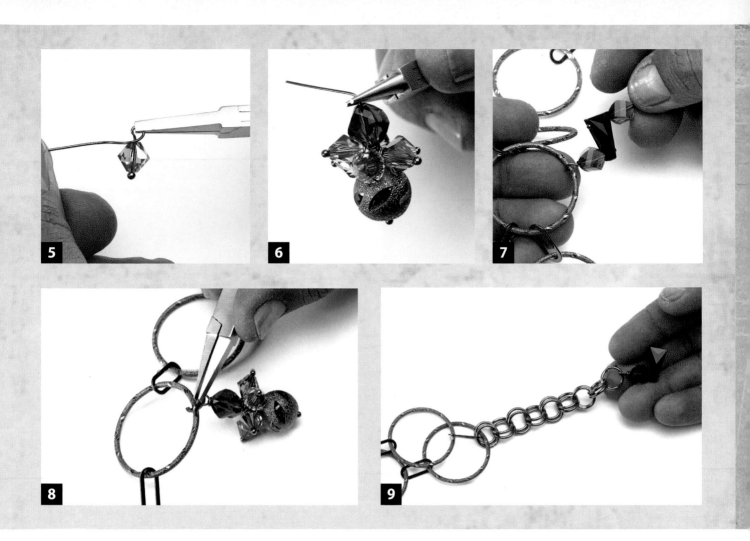

5 To make a tanzanite crystal component, string a tanzanite bead onto a ball head pin and make a wrapped loop at the other end. Make 18 of these components.

6 String the following onto a ball head pin: brushed black metal bead + 6 tanzanite crystal components + purple velvet bead. Make a simple loop with the wire at the other end of the purple velvet bead. Repeat this step 2 more times.

7 Attach the keystone links from Step 4 to the 7 center circles of the 13-link large circle chain. Carefully open the chain link and slide on the loops of the keystone link. Close the circle. Repeat this process until all 7 of the keystone links are placed inside the chain links.

8 Attach tanzanite crystal components to the 3 center circles on the 9-link large circle chain. Cut single links from the square cable chain with flush cutters to attach the components.

designer tip

As you slide the tanzanite crystal components onto the head pin, add them one at a time, and slide them on facing different directions so they lie correctly on the pin.

9 Connect 7 pairs of 12mm jump rings to the pair of jump rings at the end of the 9-link large circle chain.

Thread a ball head pin through the narrow side of a keystone bead. String on a purple velvet bead and make a wrapped loop on the other end using round-nose pliers. Attach a 12mm jump ring to the end of this component. Before closing this jump ring, attach it to the chain of jump rings on the necklace. Connect the end of this to the right side of the necklace going through the 2 oval links on the ends.

Connect a gunmetal badge clip to the chain of jump rings at the other end of the 9-link circle chain.

SOURCES Athenian Fashions Warehouse, Beadalon, Swarovski

fantasia

This silver treasure-style bracelet embraces both the colors of American flag and the workmanship of Venetian glass. The richness of the cobalt and red glass drops, the abstractionism of Venetian Klimt glass and the heavy chain add a modern touch to the Baroque feel of this link bracelet. A sassy tassel with multiple rows of chain and a rich box clasp makes for a sporty and feminine look.

MATERIALS

- 14" (35.6cm) 7.6mm silver-plated oval link cable chain
- one 3-strand sterling silver rock design box clasp
- 15" (38.1cm) 6.5mm silver-plated round link cable chain
- twelve 16mm silver-plated solid twisted rings
- six 14mm red glass discs
- six 14mm cobalt blue glass discs
- six 1.7mm satin silver cube Bead Bumpers™
- two 20mm Venetian Klimt glass shell pendants
- two 2½" (6.4cm) silver-plated fancy head pins

- two 10mm Venetian Klimt glass cube beads
- one 26mm red glass disco ball pendant
- one 26mm cobalt blue glass disco ball pendant
- 21" (53.3cm) sterling silver small cable chain
- two silver-plated modern flower bead caps
- 5" (12.7cm) 20-gauge silver-plated German style round wire
- one Swarovski Elements 10mm dark indigo round bead *Article 5000*
- one 4mm sterling silver smooth rondelle

TOOLS

- flush cutters
- round-nose pliers
- two flat-nose pliers

variation *Love the bracelet but feel that it's too much for your wrist? Make this pair of demure crystal and pearl earrings with a nautical and breezy mood. The combination of crystal caps and little potato pearls will be a staple in your jewelry box.*

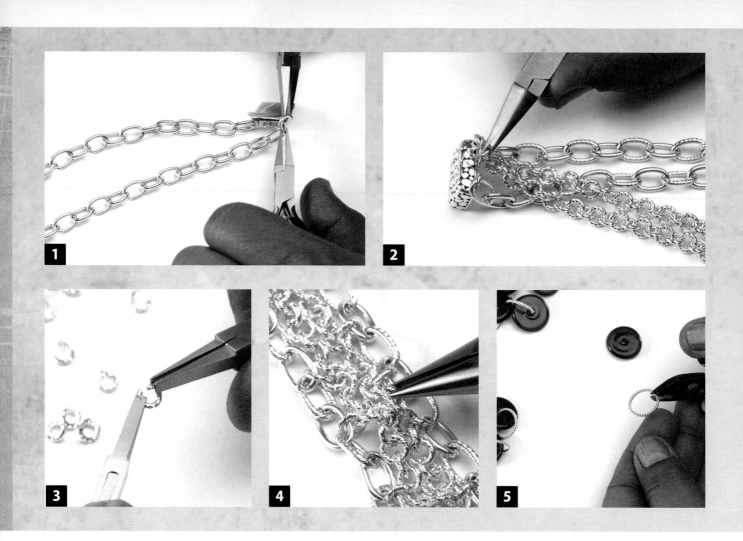

1 Cut 2 pieces of oval link cable chain into 6" (15.cm) pieces. Use 2 flat-nose pliers to open the end links of the chains and attach the links to the rings at either end of a 3-strand sterling silver box clasp. Repeat this step with the other ends of the cable chains and the other half of the box clasp.

2 Cut 2 pieces of round link cable chain into a 6" (15.2cm) piece and a 5½" (14cm) piece. Using 2 flat-nose pliers, open the end links on the ends of the chains and attach them to the center ring of the box clasp. Repeat this step with the other ends of the chains and the other half of the box clasp.

3 Open 20 links of round link cable chain and set them aside. These will be referred to as jump rings in the remaining steps.

4 Attach the 2 pieces of round link cable chain together to make a center chain, using 6 pre-opened jump rings. Space the jump rings evenly throughout the length of the chain.

Attach the large cable chains on either side of the bracelet to the center chain using 7 pre-opened jump rings on each side.

5 Cut a solid twisted ring and slide on a red glass disc. Repeat this step to make 6 red glass disc components and 6 blue glass disc components.

6 Feed a Bead Bumper and a shell pendant onto an ornate head pin and make a wrapped loop on top of the bead. Repeat this step 5 more times with another glass shell, 2 glass cubes, a red disco ball bead and a blue disco ball bead.

7 Make a tassel by cutting sterling silver small cable chain into 19 pieces approximately 1¼" (3.2cm) each. Fold down the petals of 2 silver-plated bead caps. Attach a chain piece onto each hole on a bead cap by opening the end link, sliding it through the hole and then closing the link.

8 Make a large half loop at the end of a 3" (7.6cm) piece of German style wire. Slide the end links of the remaining pieces of chain from Step 7 onto this loop. Complete the loop and wrap the excess wire around the base of the loop once. Trim the excess wire.

9 Slide the bead cap with chain pieces onto the wire with the petals facing toward the loop. Slide the empty bead cap onto the wire with the petals facing away from the loop. Slide a dark indigo round bead and a sterling silver rondelle onto the wire and make another loop on top of the bead.

10 Attach the components made in Steps 5–6 to 1 side of the bracelet in the following pattern, using the jump rings from Step 3: blue disc + red disc + glass shell + blue disc + red disc + blue disc + red disco ball + glass cube + red disc. Attach blue and red glass discs directly to the chain, opening and closing the solid twisted rings. Use jump rings opened in Step 3 to attach all the other components, including the tassel, which is attached to the ornate side of the box clasp.

Repeat same pattern in reverse on the other side of the bracelet.

SOURCES Beadalon, Elvee/Rosenberg, Murano Glass Beads

dazzling retro

I am attracted to the clean geometry of everything Art Deco, and with this project, I wanted to echo retro Hollywood glamour with accents of black-and-white Lucite and a touch of crystal to emphasize its timeless appeal. The acrylic chain is a nice surprise because, although this piece looks heavy, it will feel light and comfortable around the neck. Wear it with a sophisticated suit and feel like a million dollars!

MATERIALS

- four Swarovski Elements 10mm crystal buttons *Article 5328*
- four BeadFix™ adhesive squares
- two 30mm white Lucite flat coin beads
- 24" (61cm) 20-gauge silver-plated German style wire
- four silver color large Lucite flower bead caps
- two 25mm black Lucite round beads
- two 20mm × 28mm black/silver oval Lucite beads
- four 9mm silver-plated pinch bail pendants
- four 20mm × 45mm clear Lucite Art Deco pendants
- two silver-plated crimp covers
- two Swarovski Elements 8mm crystal rondelles *Article 5020*
- two 15mm × 20mm silver color large Lucite cylinder beads
- eight 4mm silver-plated jump rings
- four 8mm silver-plated jump rings
- two silver-plated toggle bars from a 16.8mm toggle clasp
- two 14mm × 23mm white rectangle Lucite chain links with connectable slits
- eighteen 14mm × 23mm black rectangle Lucite chain links with connectable slits
- two 18mm × 40mm white oval Lucite chain links with connectable slits
- two 18mm × 40mm black oval Lucite chain links with connectable slits

TOOLS

- chain-nose pliers
- curved squeeze scissors
- flush cutters
- pencil
- round-nose pliers

1 Using flush cutters, cut the loops off 4 10mm crystal buttons, as flush as possible to the back surface.

2 Place a button onto the paper side of an adhesive square and trace around it with a pencil. Cut the adhesive square just inside the pencil outline. Carefully remove a protective backing from the cut square and apply the sticky side to the back of the button, pressing firmly. Remove the backing from the exposed side of the adhesive square and firmly press onto the center of a 30mm white Lucite flat coin bead. Repeat this step 3 more times so both sides of 2 white Lucite coin beads have buttons.

3 Cut a 4" (10.2cm) piece of German style wire. Make a wrapped loop at the end with round-nose pliers and cut the excess wire. String a white Lucite coin bead with buttons onto the wire and then make a wrapped loop at the end. Repeat this step for the other white Lucite coin bead.

4 Cut a 4" (10.2cm) piece of German style wire. Make a wrapped loop at the end with round-nose pliers and cut the excess wire. String on the following: bead cap + 25mm black Lucite round bead + bead cap. Make a wrapped loop at the end. Repeat this step to make a 2nd black Lucite component.

5 Cut a 4" (10.2cm) piece of German style wire. Make a wrapped loop at the end with round-nose pliers and cut the excess wire. String a 20mm × 28mm black/silver oval Lucite bead onto the wire and then make a wrapped loop at the end. Repeat this step to make a 2nd black/silver oval component.

designer tip

If necessary, file the crystal buttons flat with a nail file before adhering.

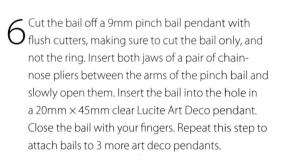

6 Cut the bail off a 9mm pinch bail pendant with flush cutters, making sure to cut the bail only, and not the ring. Insert both jaws of a pair of chain-nose pliers between the arms of the pinch bail and slowly open them. Insert the bail into the hole in a 20mm × 45mm clear Lucite Art Deco pendant. Close the bail with your fingers. Repeat this step to attach bails to 3 more art deco pendants.

7 Attach 2 Art Deco pendants to a loop on a white Lucite coin bead component (from Step 3) with 2 4mm jump rings.

8 Attach a black Lucite component (from Step 4) to the other loop in the white Lucite coin bead component with a 4mm jump ring. Connect a black/silver oval component (from Step 5) to the other loop in the black Lucite component with a 4mm jump ring.

9 Repeat Steps 7–8 to make a 2nd Art Deco dangling component, and then set these components aside.

10 Cut a 5" (12.7cm) piece of German style wire. Make a wrapped loop at the end with round-nose pliers and cut the excess wire. String on the following: closed crimp cover + 8mm crystal rondelle + 2 15mm × 20mm silver color Lucite cylinder beads + 8mm crystal rondelle + closed crimp cover. Make a wrapped loop at the end and trim the excess wire.

11 Attach an Art Deco dangling component (from Steps 7–8) to the end of the cylinder bead component (from in Step 10) with a 4mm jump ring. Repeat this step to attach the other Art Deco dangling component to the other end of the cylinder bead component.

12 Attach 2 8mm jump rings to the loops on each end of the cylinder bead component. Attach a silver-plated toggle bar to the 2nd jump ring on each end.

13 Connect Lucite chain links to each other as follows: white rectangle + black rectangle + black oval + white oval + 8 black rectangles. Reverse this pattern to finish the rest of the chain section.

14 Use the toggle bars on the cylinder bead component to connect the Lucite chain to the rest of the necklace by sliding them through the links.

SOURCES Beadalon, Elvee/Rosenberg, Swarovski

netted choker

This design was born from experimenting with the stretchiness of beading wire. I wanted to explore the innate properties of beading wire and its ability to maintain its shape. I was surprised by the visual impact the wire created and the semicircles that were produced. Assembling this choker does require patience as you adjust the positions of the wire duets, but the end result is simply stunning. I hope you enjoy creating and wearing this striking choker as much as I enjoyed designing it.

MATERIALS

- 36" (91.4cm) 7-strand 0.24" (6.1mm) copper color wire
- seven #3 crimp tubes
- twelve #2 crimp tubes
- twelve silver-plated loop crimps
- thirteen 4mm copper crimp covers
- six 4mm silver-plated crimp covers

- twelve 4mm silver plated jump rings
- six Swarovski Elements 11mm × 5.5mm mocha briolette pendants *Article 6010*
- six Swarovski Elements 11mm × 5.5mm Indian pink briolette pendants *Article 6010*
- two sets of silver-plated crimp hooks and eyes

TOOLS

- chain-nose pliers
- flush cutters
- Mighty Crimper Tool
- standard crimp tool

à la mode *Explore the intensity of a diagonal print by wearing a zebra-print dress with your unique choker. Instead of traditional black and white, find one with brown and white stripes. Wow your friends by topping it off with leather pink stilettos to coordinate with those pink crystal briolettes. Add an oversized pink Peruvian opal cocktail ring and be sassy!*

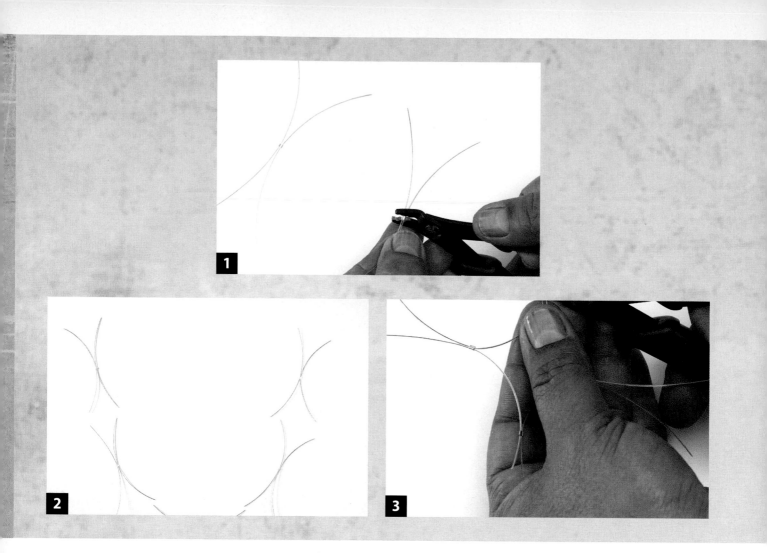

1 Cut 10 pieces of beading wire into 4" (10.2cm) lengths. Start crimping 2 pieces of wire together in the center with a #3 crimp tube, making sure the wires stay parallel to each other. Each wire should be curved away from the other. Be gentle when crimping; don't squeeze the wires in excess. Repeat this step 4 more times to make 5 wire duets.

2 Arrange the wire duets so the ends of 1 duet meet the ends of another duet. Using #2 crimp tubes, crimp the duets together at the ends, about 1½" (3.8cm) from the initial crimps from Step 1.

3 Choose a side as the bottom of the necklace. Trim the crimped wire ends on this side so 1 wire in a pair is slightly longer than the other wire. The 1st wire should be about ⅛" (3mm) long and the other should be about ¼" (6mm) long. Feed a loop crimp onto the longer wire end and crimp it into place with the outer jaw of a standard crimp tool. Feed a 2nd loop crimp onto the shorter wire end and crimp in the same way. Repeat this step until all the points on the bottom of the necklace have loop crimps.

designer tip

This choker can be an edgy accessory for a bride—just replace the crystals with colored gemstones. Morganite, kumzite, peach moonstone and chalcedony are a few among many choices.

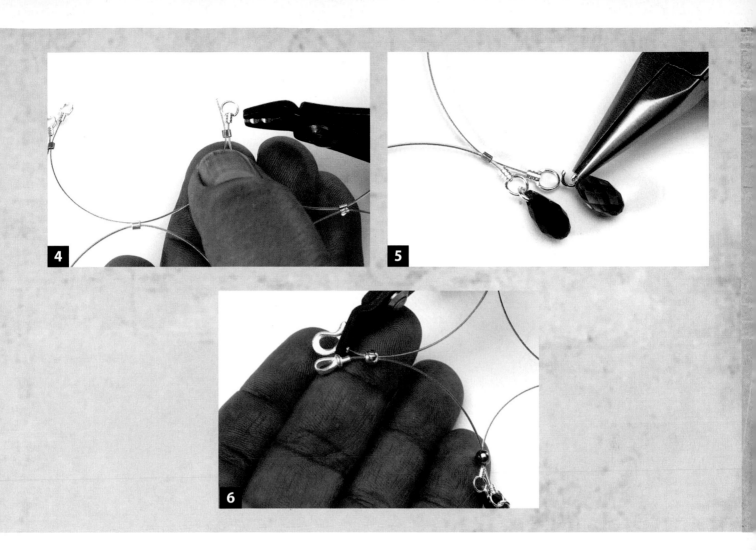

4 Cover the crimp tubes at the top and bottom points of the necklace with copper crimp covers, using the outer jaw of the Mighty Crimp Tool to close them correctly. Cover all the center crimp tubes with silver-plated crimp covers.

5 Open a 4mm jump ring and slide on a mocha briolette. Attach the jump ring with briolette to a loop crimp at an end point at the bottom of the necklace and close it gently. Open another 4mm jump ring and slide on an Indian pink briolette. Attach the jump ring and briolette to the 2nd loop crimp on the same bottom point. Repeat this step 5 times until all of the loop crimps have briolettes on them; a mocha briolette and a pink briolette should be on each point.

6 Trim the wires at the ends of the necklace to approximately ½" (1.3cm). Crimp a hook and an eye onto the pairs of wires at each end of the necklace with the Mighty Crimper Tool.

variation *Mimic the shape of the Netted Choker by using four-way square connectors, 4mm jump rings, briolettes from the necklace and modern ear wires. Attach a briolette to the top and bottom connectors. Make a second earring by switching the positions of briolettes for an extra pizzazz.*

SOURCES Beadalon, Swarovski

brighter than light

It's time to shine!

Jewelry has become one of the most powerful expressions of personal style, and in answer to today's intense quest for individuality, Swarovski Elements, Swarovski's product brand for cut crystal components, fulfills the desire in all of us to create our own personal crystal style. This extensive collection of crystal beads, pendants, trims and more is enhanced and updated twice a year and comes in many shapes, sizes, colors and effects.

With the company's long history of collaboration with the world's leading designers and couturiers, Swarovski Elements understands the creative process involved in using crystal to bring highly individual visions to life. I am proud to be able to pass these visions on to you. Using a fashion-forward approach, I designed very distinctive jewelry pieces for this chapter.

CHAPTER 3

I pay homage to my homeland with *Terra Brasilis* (see page 60), which showcases an intricate use of stringing wire, box chain and crystals. *Back to the Future* (see page 64) mixes hardware paraphernalia with strands of crystal beads inserted into clear tubing to create a futuristic choker. For a sassy and romantic look, try making *Bougainvillea* (see page 70), a luscious red-and-pink necklace that blends edginess with post-hippie style, creating a vibrant and sensual neckline contour. And you will be enchanted by the easy-going mood of the *Pendulum* earrings (see page 74), which feature an ultra-modern wire-wrapping technique.

All of these designs can be assembled with any crystal brand of your preference, but I believe that only Swarovski Elements produces maximum light refraction and perfection in cut, luxury and prestige that suits my design ambitions. The use of crystals in the do-it-yourself jewelry market is an affordable way to add bling to complement an outfit. It's instant glamour!

terra brasilis

The existence of a large, varied bird population in the Brazilian Amazon and its numerous indigenous tribes inspired me to create this feather-like necklace. This piece is a homage to my homeland and its rich cultural background. By combining three different colors of stringing wire, a stainless steel box chain and an assortment of crystals, I mimic the artistic and unparalleled work of the Amazonian tribes and the spirit of a tropical nation.

~ For Ubirajara.

MATERIALS

- 36" (91.4cm) 19-strand .012" (0.3mm) silver-plated bead stringing wire
- 36" (91.4cm) 19-strand .012" (0.3mm) satin copper bead stringing wire
- 36" (91.4cm) 19-strand .012" (0.3mm) satin silver bead stringing wire
- 20" (50.8cm) stainless steel small box chain
- thirty-six #2 silver-plated crimp tubes
- seventy-two #1 silver-plated crimp tubes
- two silver-plated medium pinch bail pendants

- 6" (15.2cm) 18-gauge sterling silver half-hard round wire
- two 4mm jump rings
- three 6mm jump rings
- one stainless steel lobster clasp

SWAROVSKI ELEMENTS

- twenty-four 4mm olivine satin bicone beads *Article 5301*
- four 4mm jonquil bicone beads *Article 5301*
- twenty 5mm lime bicone beads *Article 5301*
- seventeen 4mm citrine Xilion beads *Article 5328*
- two 32mm × 20mm emerald leaf pendants *Article 6735*

TOOLS

- chain-nose pliers
- flush cutters
- round-nose pliers
- standard crimp tool

variation *For a head to toe Brazilian makeover, consider a luscious gold palette using gold box chain mixed with special effect crystal shades. Finish it off using square crystal frames as your focal point for a more urban look.*

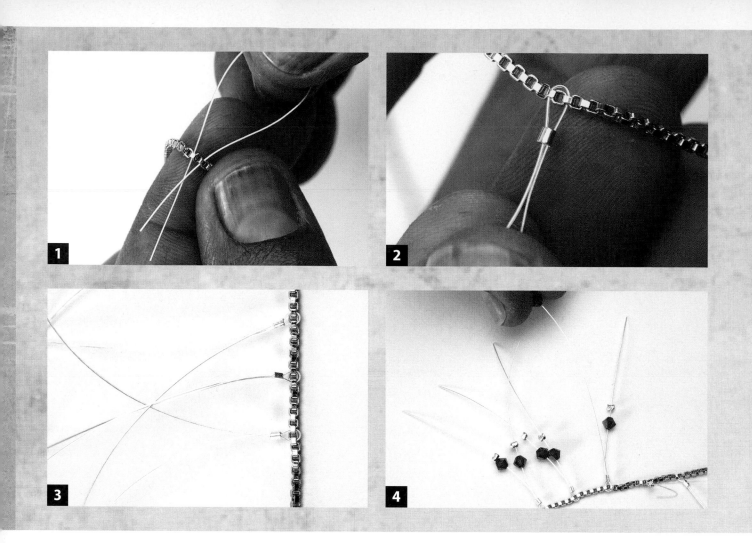

1 Cut 12 pieces of silver-plated beading wire, 12 pieces of satin copper wire and 12 pieces of satin silver wire, all 4" (10.2cm) in length. Separate the pieces by color.

Find the center of a 20" (50.8cm) piece of stainless steel box chain. Thread a 4" (10.2cm) piece of silver-plated wire through the chain, 2 links to the left of the center. Thread the other end of the wire through the chain, 2 links to the right of the 1st link. Pull both ends through so the ends of the wire are even.

2 Using the standard crimp tool, crimp a #2 crimp tube around both ends of the wire, as close to the chain as possible.

3 Continue adding 4" (10.2cm) pieces of wire to the chain as described in Steps 1 and 2, spacing each piece 4 links apart, using the following pattern and working up the left side of the necklace: 3 sterling silver wires, 3 satin copper wires, 3 satin silver wires. Repeat this pattern once more. Add 4" (10.2cm) wires to the right side of the necklace, following the same pattern.

4 String an olivine crystal onto each silver-plated wire end and attach a #1 crimp tube at the end, leaving about ⅛" (3mm) of excess wire at the ends. Repeat this step using lime crystals on the satin copper wires and citrine crystals on the satin silver wires.

designer tip

Crimp each wire close to the box chain, and make sure the wire goes around the proper vertical link so that all the ends are pointing in the same direction.

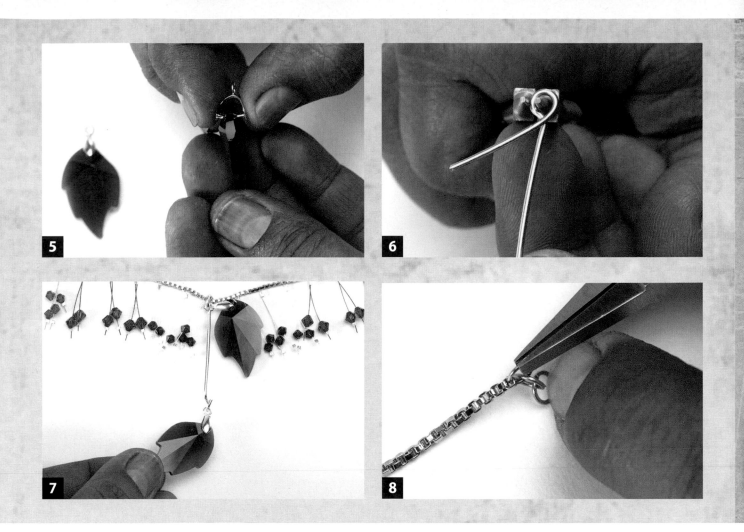

5 Cut off the top bail of a pinch bail pendant. Open the bail wide enough to close around the holes of a crystal leaf. Repeat this step to connect a pinch bail pendant to a 2nd crystal leaf.

6 Make a simple loop at the end of a 6" (15.2cm) piece of 18-gauge sterling silver wire. Make a 2nd simple loop 1½" (3.8cm) from the 1st loop. Trim any excess wire.

7 Open 1 loop in the 18-gauge wire from Step 6 and attach it to the center of the necklace. Before closing, slide on a leaf component from Step 5 and then close the loop. Open the other loop in the wire and slide on the other leaf component. Close the loop.

8 Connect a 4mm jump ring to 1 end of the necklace. Connect a 6mm jump ring to the 4mm jump ring, and slide on the nonopening end of a lobster clasp. Repeat this step on the other end of the necklace, sliding on the opening part of the clasp.

SOURCES Beadalon, Swarovski

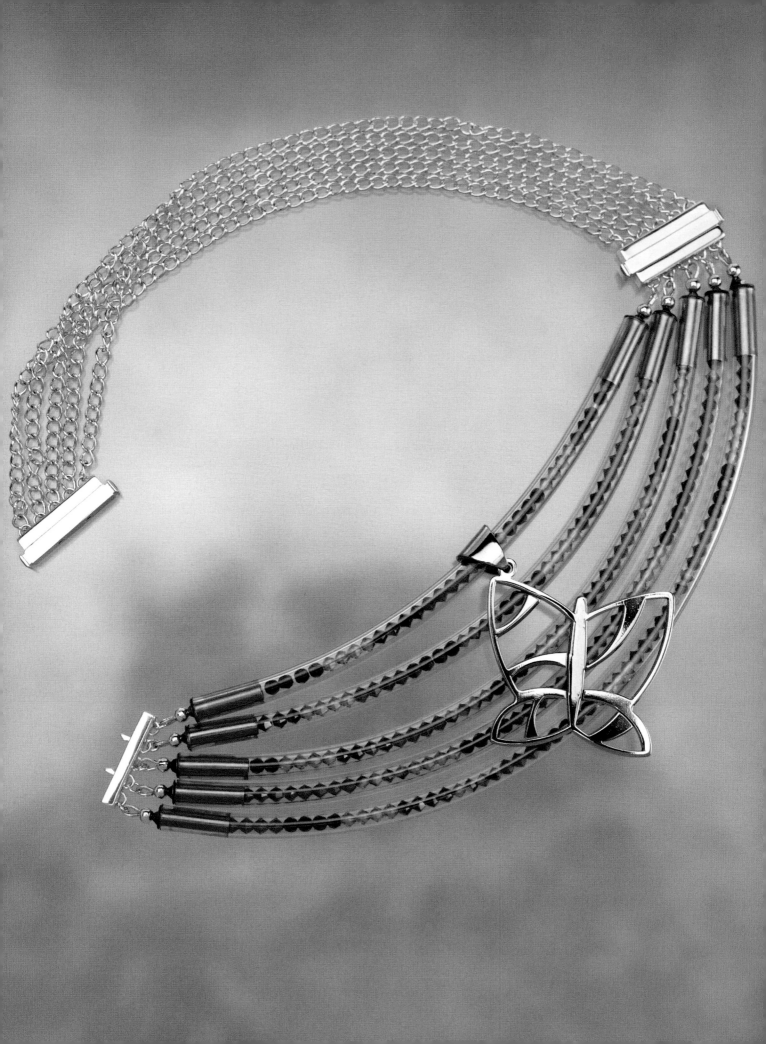

back to the future

Many years ago, I was awed by a piece made by a Bulgarian designer. He had created a bracelet that combined clear plastic tubing with fancy stones. I used similar elements when designing Back to the Future, a necklace reminiscent of 1970s science-fiction movies. A modern clasp and a butterfly pendant play a major role in this design and are the perfect finishing touch.

~ For Nik Sardamov.

MATERIALS

- 36" (91.4cm) ¼" × .17" (6mm × 4mm) clear vinyl tubing

- ten brass tubing inserts for ¼" (6mm) tubing

- 10" (3m) 49-strand .024" (6mm) silver-plated stringing wire

- ten #2 silver-plated crimp tubes

- ten sterling silver large Wire Guardians™

- two sterling silver 5-strand rectangular mechanical clasps

- ten 3mm silver-plated crimp covers

- one large stainless steel modern butterfly pendant with gold-plated accent

- 5' (1.5m) sterling silver medium curb chain

- ten 4mm sterling silver jump rings

SWAROVSKI ELEMENTS

- fifty 3mm crystal metallic blue 2X Xilion beads *Article 5328*

- fifty 3mm indicolite Xilion beads *Article 5328*

- fifty 3mm dark indigo round beads *Article 5000*

- fifty 3mm palace green opal Xilion beads *Article 5328*

- fifty 3mm white opal sky blue Xilion beads *Article 5328*

TOOLS

- chain-nose pliers

- flush cutters

- Mighty Crimper Tool

- scissors

- standard crimp tool

à la mode   *The dash of futurism from this choker complements well an effervescent green pencil skirt. An off-white corset with geometric lines emphasizes the necklace's theme, while a pair of sateen gladiator sandals adds trendiness. Add a showerhead white opal cocktail ring for extra drama. Very chic!*

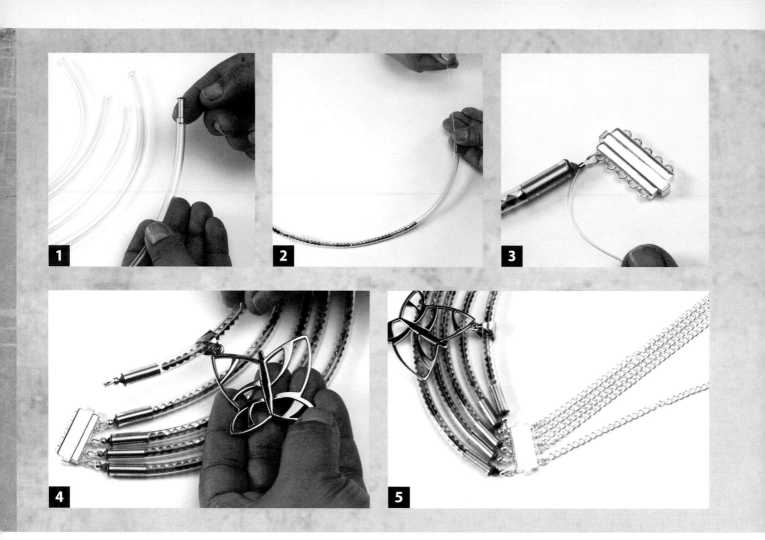

1 Using sharp scissors, cut 5 pieces of clear vinyl tubing, making clean right-angle cuts, into the following lengths: 7" (17.8cm), 7¼" (18.4cm), 8¼" (21cm), 9" (22.9cm) and 9 ⅞" (25.1cm). Insert a brass insert into 1 end of each tube.

2 Cut a 20" (50.8cm) piece of silver-plated stringing wire and tie a double overhand knot 3" (7.6cm) from the end. String on the following beads: 4 crystal metallic + 4 indicolite + 4 dark indigo + 4 palace green + 4 white opal. Continue this pattern until 56 beads have been strung. Insert the end of the wire without the knot into the 9 ⅞" (25.1cm) piece of tubing, at the end without the brass insert. Pull the wire through and carefully guide the beads into the tube.

3 Once all the beads are inside the tubing, insert a brass end into the other end of the tube. String the following onto the end of the wire: indicolite + crimp tube + Wire Guardian. Attach the Wire Guardian with the wire in it onto an end loop on

a sterling silver 5-strand rectangular clasp. Feed the wire back through the crimp bead, pull the excess slack and crimp the tube. Cover the crimp tube with a crimp cover. Connect the other end of the tube to a 2nd rectangular clasp in the same way.

4 Repeat Steps 2–3, working from the longest to the shortest tube, alternating the sequence of bead colors to achieve color depth. You will need to adjust the number of beads for each tube. Before connecting the shortest strand to the 2nd rectangular clasp, slide on a butterfly pendant.

5 Cut curb chain into the following lengths: 7¼" (18.4cm), 7½" (19.1cm), 8½" (22cm), 9¼" (23.5cm) and 9½" (24.1cm). Connect each piece of chain to a loop on a rectangular clasp by opening the end link of the chain piece and attaching it to the loop. Attach the other end of each piece of chain to the corresponding loop at the other side of the necklace.

SOURCES Artbeads, Beadalon, Swarovski

luxurious hoops

These glamorous and femme fatale earrings are so easy to make, you'll want to make a pair for everyone you know. They are perfect for wearing to a wedding, a prom or a ball at the White House . . . you never know, it could happen! These earrings will add equal elegance to a flowery summer dress or a satin ballroom gown.

MATERIALS

- 2' (70cm) 19-strand .018 blue stringing wire
- two #4 silver-plated crimp tubes
- two 7mm silver-plated sparkle crimp covers
- two 6mm silver-plated jump rings
- two back loop ear wires

SWAROVSKI ELEMENTS

- 5" (12.7cm) aquamarine crystal mesh *Article 55000*

TOOLS

- chain-nose pliers
- flush cutters
- Mighty Crimper Tool

à la mode
A sheer light blue gouache dress captures the loose and flowing essence of these hoops. Wear it with silver sandals and straight hair for a look of pure serenity.

1 Using flush cutters, cut a piece of aquamarine mesh into a 5 stone × 17 stone rectangle. Trim around the rectangle to create clean edges, cutting carefully so that the back prongs are not damaged during the cutting. Cut the shorter end of the rectangle into a point, and then trim again to create clean edges.

2 Carefully thread a 6" (15.2cm) piece of blue stringing wire through 5 stones at the shorter edge of the rectangle, going through all 5 stones. Thread a 2nd 6" (15.2cm) piece of blue wire through the row of 5 stones directly below. Center both wires on the rectangle.

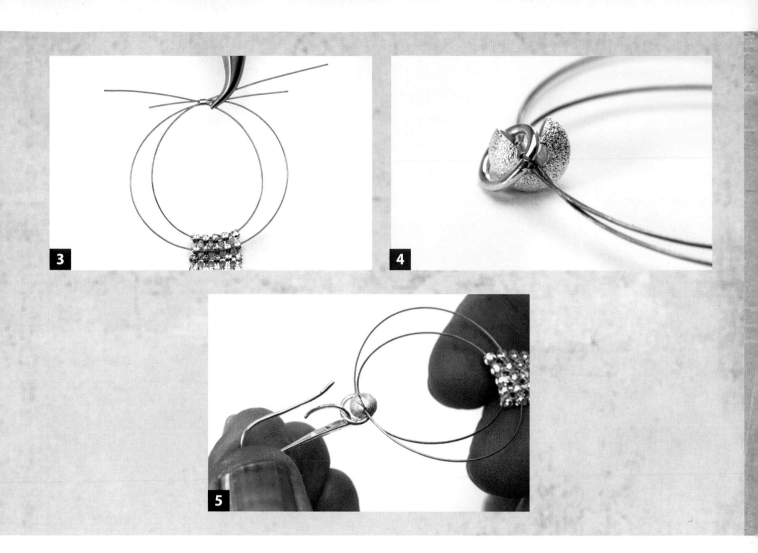

3 Curve the left ends of the 2 wires up and into a crimp tube. Do the same with the right ends, going through the opposite side of the same crimp tube so the 2 left wires intersect with the 2 right wires inside the tube. Adjust the wires to form a smaller circle inside of a slightly larger circle, and then crimp the tubes.

4 Trim the ends of the wires at the crimp tube. Cover the crimp tube with a sparkle crimp cover, but before closing, place a 6mm jump ring into the crimp cover. Use the Mighty Crimper Tool to close the crimp cover with the crimp tube and the jump ring inside.

5 Open the loop on the end of a back loop ear wire and slide on the jump ring within the crimp cover. Close the loop. Repeat Steps 1–5 for a matching earring.

designer tip

To make the wire circles the perfect size, make small adjustments before crimping. Lay the second earring over the first to make certain the circles are the same size.

SOURCES Beadalon, Swarovski

bougainvillea

This design was inspired by the cascading stems and colorful flowers of the bougainvillea plant, which is common to many tropical regions of the world. A large dream catcher wired with pink and red crystals is the main feature, but an aluminum chain mixed with pink and smoky crystal shades turns this necklace into a winning combination.

~ For Mirandulina.

MATERIALS

- sixteen 2" (5.1cm) 0.7mm silver-plated eye pins
- thirty-four 3.4mm silver-plated solid rings
- sixteen 0.6mm silver-plated barbell metal beads
- 33" (83.8cm) red color brass small cable chain
- twenty 6mm silver-plated jump rings
- 24" (61cm) 26-gauge silver-plated German style wire
- one rhodium-plated round wire dream catcher
- 16" (40.6cm) matte gray aluminum double curb chain
- eighteen 8mm rhodium-plated jump rings
- one medium pinch bail
- four 2" (5.1cm) 0.7mm silver-plated ball head pins
- six 4mm silver-plated jump rings
- one sterling silver red/mother of pearl hand-laid mosaic toggle clasp

SWAROVSKI ELEMENTS

- ten 6mm greige cube beads *Article 5601*
- eight 6mm Indian red round beads *Article 5000*
- sixteen 6mm greige bicone pendants *Article 5601*
- nine 11mm × 5.5mm padparadscha briolette pendants *Article 6010*
- eight 8mm violet opal round beads *Article 5000*
- six 6mm rose Xilion beads *Article 5328*
- twelve 6mm light gray opal bicone pendants *Article 5601*
- ten 13mm × 6.5mm crystal silver shade briolette pendants *Article 6010*
- ten 4mm indian red Xilion beads *Article 5328*
- twelve 4mm indian pink Xilion beads *Article 5328*
- one 40mm crystal red magma coral pendant *Article 6790*

TOOLS

- chain-nose pliers
- flush cutter
- jump ring opener
- round-nose pliers

à la mode

A very girly necklace full of reds and pinks calls for an equally girly outfit, so try a rich red strapless dress worn with neutral leather wedged sandals. Finish it off with a slightly asymmetrical hair updo and be ready for a Sunday brunch or a wedding on the beach.

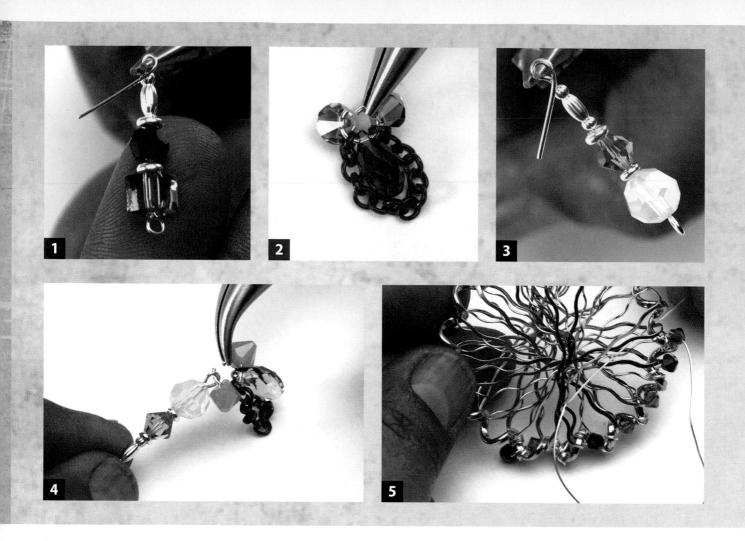

1 String the following onto an eye pin: 6mm greige cube bead + 3.4mm solid ring + 6mm Indian red bead + 3.4mm solid ring + barbell bead. Make a matching loop at the end of the pin with round-nose pliers, and then cut the excess wire. Make 8 of these components.

2 Cut 8 pieces of red chain, each 14 links long. Slide the following onto a 6mm jump ring: 6mm greige bicone pendant + the end link of a 14-link piece of red chain + 11mm × 5.5mm briolette + the other end of the 14-link piece of red chain + 6mm greige pendant. Carefully attach the jump ring to the bottom ring of a component made in Step 1. Repeat this step until all 8 components have jump rings with beads and red chain.

3 String the following onto an eye pin: 8mm violet opal + 4mm solid ring + 6mm rose + 3.4mm solid ring + barbell bead. Make a matching loop at the end of the pin with round-nose pliers and then cut the excess wire. Make 6 of these components.

4 Cut 6 pieces of red chain, each 17 links long. Slide the following onto a 6mm jump ring: 6mm light gray opal pendant + the end link of a 17-link piece of red chain + 13mm × 6.5mm briolette + the other end of the 17-link piece of red chain + 6mm light gray opal pendant. Carefully attach the jump ring to the bottom ring of a component made in Step 3. Repeat this step until all 8 components from Step 3 have jump rings with beads and red chain.

5 Cut 4 6" (15.2cm) pieces of German style wire. Wrap the end of a 6" (15.2cm) piece of wire around one of the outer points of a wire dreamcatcher. String on a 4mm Indian red bead, wrap the wire around the next outer point in the dreamcatcher 1–2 revolutions and then string on a 4mm Indian pink bead. Repeat this step, alternating between red and pink beads until every point on the dreamcatcher has a bead. Begin with a new 6" (15.2cm) piece of wire when the current wire has been completely wrapped.

6 Connect an 8" (20.3cm) piece of aluminum curb chain to the left and right sides of the dream-catcher component by sliding 2 links of the chain onto an 8mm jump ring and then attaching the jump ring to the dreamcatcher.

7 Attach the dangling components from Steps 1–2 and 3–4 onto the cable chain links on both sides of the dreamcatcher with 8mm jump rings. Attach 6 components to each side, alternating them in a pattern. Each jump ring should go through 2 links in the chain.

8 Open a pinch bail and close it around a coral branch pendant. Attach an 8mm jump ring to the bail. Attach the entire component to the bottom center of the dreamcatcher. Attach the remaining 2 dangling components on either side of the coral branch pendant.

9 Cut lengths of red chain in random lengths. String leftover beads onto head pins and attach the wires to the chains by looping the ends of the head pins into the chain. Attach these components randomly to the bottom of the dreamcatcher.

10 Attach an 8mm jump ring through 2 links of chain on each end of the necklace. Attach a 4mm jump ring to each 8mm jump ring. Attach the toggle ring to the 4mm jump ring on 1 end of the necklace and the toggle bar to the other end.

SOURCES Athenian Fashions Warehouse, Beadalon, Swarovski

pendulum

Wire wrapping is one of the most popular jewelry-making techniques. I wanted to make a fresh piece that employed wire-wrapping that hadn't been done before. This project explores the geometry of the focal crystal bead, with the wire sculpted around its lines. The result is an almost-hoop style earring with lots of movement and drama.

MATERIALS

- 36" (91.4cm) 22-gauge silver-plated German style wire
- two 4mm silver-plated jump rings
- two silver-plated oval hinged ear posts
- two Paula Radke Dichroic 6mm cobalt blue dichroic disc beads

SWAROVSKI ELEMENTS

- two 18mm indicolite graphic beads *Article 5520*

TOOLS

- chain-nose pliers
- flush cutters
- round-nose pliers

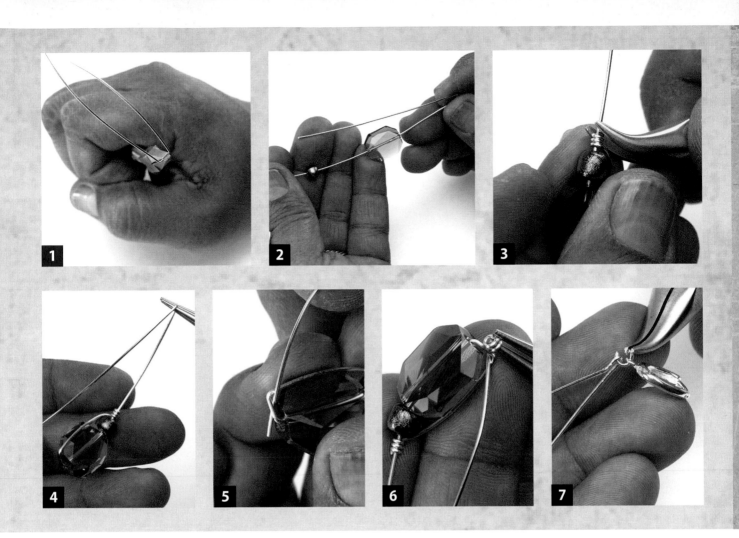

1 Cut a 9" (22.9cm) piece of German style wire. Using chain-nose pliers, pinch the wire about 3" (7.6cm) from the end. Bend the wire at the chain-nose pliers to form a U shape.

2 String a graphic bead and a dichroic bead onto the longer portion of the wire.

3 Carefully bend the short portion of the wire up along the side of the graphic bead and the dichroic bead. Wrap the shorter portion of wire around the longer portion tightly, making 3 full revolutions. Trim the excess wire and tuck in the end.

4 Using round-nose pliers, grasp the longer portion of the wire about 1½" (3.8cm) above the dichroic bead. Bend the wire at the round-nose pliers, making the bend wide enough to attach a 4mm jump ring to it.

5 Carefully slide the end of the wire through the loop at the bottom of the graphic bead. Bend the wire upward and away from the bead at a 45-degree angle.

6 Grasp the wire where it extends from the loop with round-nose pliers. Carefully wrap the wire around 1 tip of the pliers, forming an upside-down corkscrew. Wrap the wire around the tip 4 full revolutions. Remove the pliers and cut the excess wire. Close the corkscrew by squeezing it top-to-bottom with the chain-nose pliers until each corkscrew revolution is flush with the next.

7 Squeeze the top bend in the earring slightly, using the tip of the round-nose pliers, to accommodate the ear post. Attach a 4mm jump ring to the top of the earring. Attach a hinged ear post to the jump ring. Repeat Steps 1–6 to make a 2nd earring.

SOURCES Beadalon, Paula Radke Dichroic, Swarovski

quicksilver

I am attracted to shiny surfaces. To me, sterling silver and gold are the most beautiful precious metals, as long as they're clean and polished. These days, oxidized metals, tarnished silver, antique gold and brass and copper patina are all "in," but I still argue that sterling silver and gold remain the two most popular and timeless shades of precious metal. I also appreciate beads and findings with shimmering, polished and glowing surfaces.

For this chapter, I wanted the metallic element to be the focus. To celebrate "de '80s," I created *Limoncello* (see page 78), a beaded necklace featuring large silver-plated abacus beads, lime green faux Murano glass and acid green aluminum chain. The combination of these odd geometric shapes is strikingly eccentric. The *Dotted Dome Cuff* (see page 80) is an eye-catching piece that is also easy to assemble. It is made up of distinctive sterling silver connectors held together by jump rings and finished off with flatback crystals. I blended several different

components to achieve a metallic look in *Mirrored Peacock* (see page 83). In this project, you can practice your wire-looping skills to create a fringe of bugle beads and a linked strand of freshwater pearls. The centerpiece is a ladder of glass peacock beads, which produces a quivering motion, reflecting faint light.

After working with copper sheet for the first time, I designed an Yves Saint Laurent-inspired necklace that is a fashion statement on its own—bold, substantial and chic! *Monsieur Laurent* (see page 86) will provide you with a dash of French nostalgia and glamour.

The designs in this chapter will garner admiring glances and covetous "Where did you get that?" inquiries. The fashion sketches are there to guide you in your clothing choices, but if you are afraid to take a risk, remember that a black outfit will suit any of these designs. Either way, I guarantee you won't be lacking in elegance.

limoncello

On a trip to Tuscany, I tried limoncello for the first time. When I found these lemon-colored glass drops, I knew I had to incorporate them into a piece of jewelry that was reminiscent of the sweet lemony beverage. The sleek drops and polished metallic discs, combined with chunky chain and geometric beads, result in a visually strong necklace that makes a dramatic statement. The mixture of pop culture, updated 1980s retro, punk and hip-hop really pops!

MATERIALS

- 18" (45.7cm) 12mm lemon aluminum cable chain
- 20" (50.8cm) 19-strand .024" (0.6mm) satin silver bright bead stringing wire
- two #3 silver-plated crimp tubes
- two 8mm rhodium-plated jump rings
- two 4mm silver-plated lined crimp covers
- nine 11mm × 30mm yellow Chinese glass teardrop beads
- ten 6mm black-base green dichroic glass beads
- two Swarovski Elements 10mm jet Helix beads *Article 5020*
- nine Swarovski Elements 6mm jet sew-on stones *Article 3400*
- four 18mm silver-plated deco cube beads
- six 30mm silver-plated double cone beads with large holes
- three Swarovski Elements 10mm jet Xilion beads *Article 5320*
- one medium green dichroic square donut
- one large antique silver bar from a 28mm toggle clasp
- one 2" (5.1cm) silver-plated ball head pin

TOOLS

- chain-nose pliers
- flush cutters
- Mighty Crimper Tool
- nylon jaw chain-nose pliers
- round-nose pliers
- standard crimp tool

1 Using nylon jaw chain-nose pliers, separate a piece of lemon cable chain 7 links long. Open the 7th link and connect it to the 1st ring. Make 4 of these components.

Separate an 8-link piece of lemon cable chain and connect the 8th link to the 1st link. Make 2 of these components.

2 Thread the end of an 18" (45.7cm) piece of 19-strand bead stringing wire through a #3 crimp tube and a 8mm jump ring, and then back through the crimp tube. Crimp the tube with the standard crimp tool. Carefully cover the crimp tube with a crimp cover and close it with the outer jaw of the Mighty Crimper Tool.

3 String the following onto the wire: teardrop, small end 1st + dichroic + Helix + 7-link chain component (from Step 1) + sew-on stone + deco cube + sew-on stone + dichroic + teardrop, large end 1st + double cone + 7-link chain component + Xilion + double cone + teardrop, small end 1st + 7-link chain component + sew-on stone + dichroic + deco cube + sew-on stone + dichroic + teardrop, large end 1st + double cone + 7-link chain component + Xilion + double cone. Continue

this pattern in reverse to create the opposite side of the necklace.

4 Once all the beads and components are placed, finish the end as in Step 2 with a #3 crimp tube, a 8mm jump ring and a crimp cover. Attach a dichroic donut to this jump ring. Attach a toggle bar to the jump ring on the other end of the necklace.

5 String the following onto a 2" (5.1cm) ball head pin: sew-on stone + teardrop, large end 1st. Make a simple loop at the end and attach the loop to a 16-link piece of lemon cable chain. Open the end link of the chain and wrap it around the center of the necklace, between the 2 center double cone beads. Attach the end link to the 8th link of the chain to connect it to the necklace. Carefully close the link. Wear this *Limoncello* like you were born in Italy!

designer tip

If you're more like an owl than a canary, try a jet black-and-gunmetal palette and get ready to rock on!

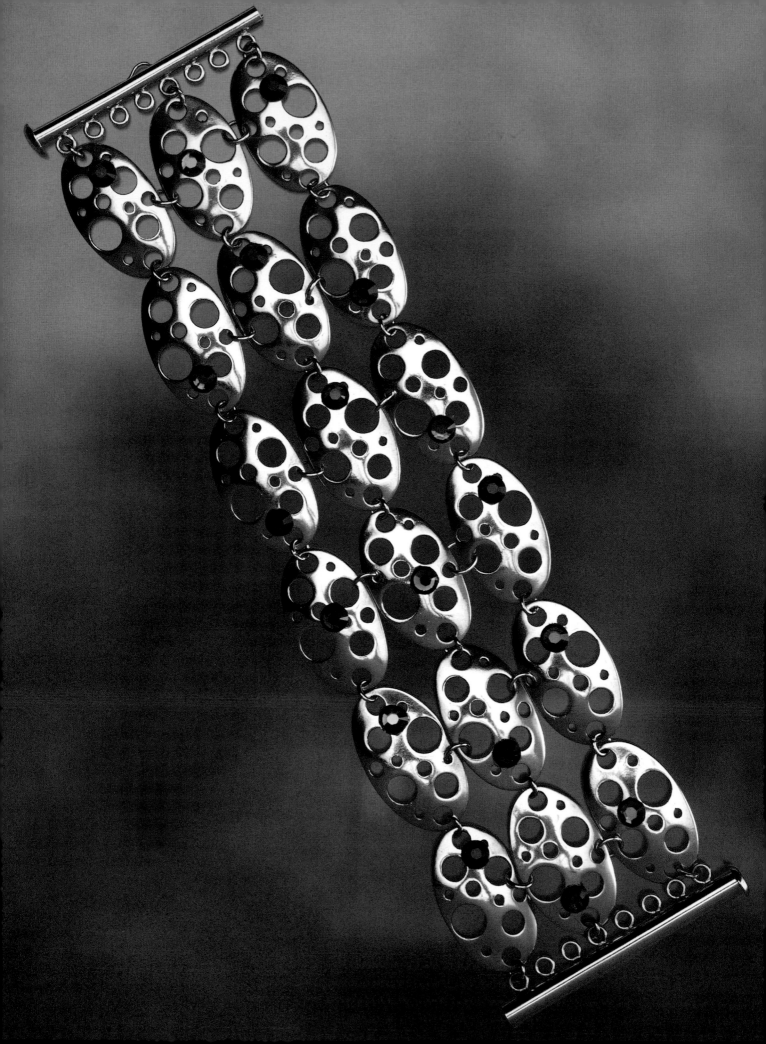

dotted dome cuff

Allured by the shape and texture of these oval-shaped sterling silver components, I created a cuff that highlights their striking look. Flat crystal stones add extra sparkle and draw attention to the cuff's versatile outline. This is a stress-free, airy and eye-catching design, perfect to assemble during a relaxing afternoon.

MATERIALS

- twenty-one 4mm sterling silver jump rings
- one set sterling silver 8-ring slide clasp
- eighteen 15mm × 25mm sterling silver oval dome connectors with holes
- twelve 6mm sterling silver jump rings
- six Swarovski Elements 20ss foiled montana flatback stones *Article 2028*
- six Swarovski Elements 20ss foiled siam flatback stones *Article 2028*
- six Swarovski Elements 20ss foiled smoked topaz flatback stones *Article 2028*
- three BeadFix™ adhesive squares

TOOLS

- Curved Squeeze Scissors
- straight pin
- two chain-nose pliers

à la mode
When wearing the Dotted Dome Cuff, *take some cues from the outfit paired with the* Back to the Future *necklace (see page 64). Trade in the green pencil skirt for one in black and add a pair of slim dangling earrings. A bare neck makes for a knock-out look. Fabulous!*

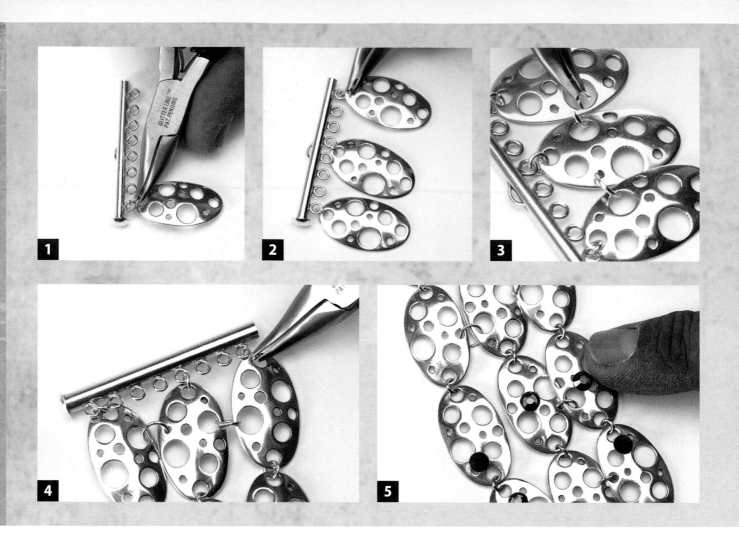

1 Open a 4mm jump ring and attach it to the end ring of a silver slide clasp and a hole in an oval silver component. Close the jump ring gently.

2 Attach an oval dome connector to the 5th and 8th rings on the bar clasp with 4mm jump rings.

3 Open a 6mm jump ring and attach one of the side holes of the oval component from Step 1 to a side hole of the middle oval component from Step 2. Open a 2nd 6mm jump ring and attach another side hole of the middle oval component to a side hole of the last oval component.

4 Connect the remaining oval components to the initial three to create three lengths for the bracelet. Connect the ovals together on the sides as in Step 3. Slide the slide clasp apart and attach the 2nd part to the end of the oval components in the same manner as in Step 1.

5 Press flatback stones onto the sticky side of a BeadFix adhesive square. Press forcefully to make sure the entire back of the stone is securely stuck in place. Fit several stones onto one square, and then cut around each stone using curved scissors. Peel the backing off each stone with a straight pin. Affix one stone randomly on the top surface of each oval component.

designer tip

Assembling this bracelet is fairly easy, but the placement of jump rings is tricky. Study the photos carefully to ensure you are connecting the oval components through the correct holes.

mirrored peacock

It sounds cheesy to be inspired by certain beads, but the market has been so generous lately that it's impossible not to be repeatedly amazed by certain beads. I couldn't resist the pop-art appeal of these Czech metallic peacock beads, so I created this elongated centerpiece framed by a fringe of bugle beads. I paired this with a chain of coin pearls linked by black onyx flat hexagon beads. The result is a spicy yet casually cool accessory adorned with metallic geometric accents.

MATERIALS

- 4' (1.2m) 22-gauge silver-plated German style round wire
- 7" (17.8cm) silver-plated Figaro chain
- forty-four 1.5mm black Bead Bumpers™
- fourteen 8mm–10mm green-gold freshwater pearl coin beads
- eight 6mm–7mm black onyx hexagon disc beads
- one 20mm × 20mm sterling silver square toggle clasp
- sixteen 30mm silver-lined bugle beads
- sixteen 2" (5.1cm) silver-plated ball head pins
- seven 2" (5.1cm) silver-plated eye pins
- one 20mm × 14mm green labrador peacock glass flat oval bead
- three 19mm × 12mm black labrador peacock glass rectangle beads
- three 19mm × 12mm green labrador peacock glass rectangle beads

TOOLS

- chain-nose pliers
- flush cutters
- round-nose pliers

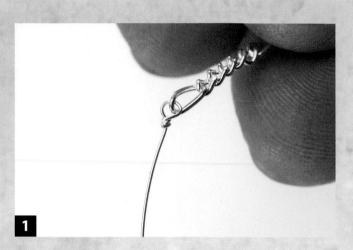

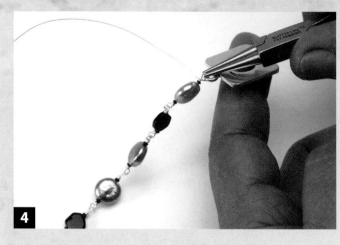

1 Using round-nose pliers, make a half loop at the end of a 10" (25.4cm) piece of German style wire. Slide on the end of a 3½" (8.9cm) piece of silver-plated Figaro chain, and then complete the loop, wrapping the wire 2 times. Trim the excess wire.

2 Thread a Bead Bumper onto the wire and slide it to the wrapped loop. String on a pearl coin bead and another Bead Bumper. Make another wrapped loop after the Bead Bumper and trim the excess wire.

3 Repeat Steps 1 and 2, replacing the pearl coin bead with a black onyx hexagon disc bead. When making the 2nd loop on this component, connect it to the loop on the pearl coin bead link. After the 1st 2 links, continue connecting pearl links and black onyx links in the following pattern: pearl + pearl + onyx + pearl + onyx + pearl + pearl + onyx + pearl. On the last pearl link, make the loop slightly larger and connect the toggle bar.

4 Repeat Steps 1–3 to create the other side of the necklace, connecting the last pearl to the toggle ring.

designer tips

• Take care not to chip the bugle beads, as they are made of glass and will chip if any pressure is put on them with pliers. Don't try to make a loop extremely close to the tip of the bead and you will be fine.

• Practice making loops to match the eye pin loops so they are consistently the same size. Fit the tips of round-nose pliers into an eye pin loop to get an idea of the perfect spot to form your loops. Mark this spot with a marker if necessary.

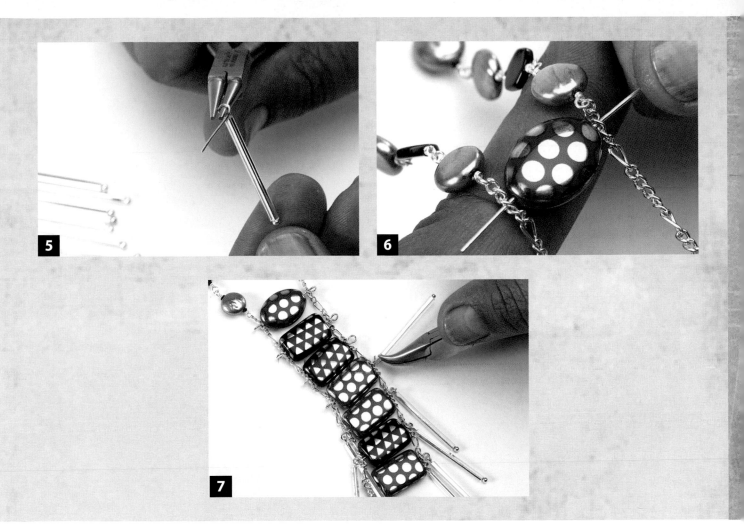

5 String a bugle bead onto a ball head pin and make a simple loop at the end with round-nose pliers, but do not close it. Trim the excess wire. Make 16 total bugle bead components.

6 Lay the sides of the necklace together, with the Figaro chains running parallel to each other. Insert an eye pin through the 3rd link of 1 chain. Slide on a green peacock oval bead. Thread the eye pin through the 3rd link in the other Figaro chain. Form a loop in the wire and trim the excess.

7 Repeat Step 6 going down the Figaro chains, using the following pattern: black peacock rectangle, black peacock rectangle, green peacock rectangle, green peacock rectangle, black peacock rectangle, green peacock rectangle. Space the rectangle beads approximately 6 links apart on each side.

Attach a bugle bead component to each of the 14 loops on the outside of the Figaro chains. Attach the final 2 bugle bead components to the end links on each of the Figaro chains.

variation *With a few more Czech bugle beads and a light blue peacock bead, you can easily create something fabulous. Use modern ear posts and you will end up with a sassy and fun pair of tassel earrings. A bit of extra zest won't hurt!*

SOURCES Beadalon, John Bead Corporation

monsieur laurent

When I was a preteen, Yves Saint-Laurent was the first fashion designer who caught my attention. I used to run to the TV anytime his name would come up in the news, eager to learn all about his latest collections. By the time my mother started wearing Opium as her number-one fragrance, I was in heaven.

This dazzling necklace is a homage to Yves Saint Laurent's visionary work. Create this astonishing pendant, encrusted with fancy stones, and celebrate fashion at its roots.

~For Kim St. Jean.

MATERIALS

- one 4" × 4" (10.2cm × 10.2cm) piece of 22-gauge copper sheet
- four 10mm silver-plated jump rings
- two Swarovski Elements 18mm × 13mm silver-foiled clear rectangle stones *Article 4610*
- two Swarovski Elements 18mm × 13mm silver-foiled erinite rectangle stones *Article 4610*
- two Swarovski Elements 18mm × 13mm silver-foiled tanzanite rectangle stones *Article 4610*
- one Swarovski Elements 20mm × 15mm silver-foiled clear rectangle stone *Article 4610*
- one Swarovski Elements 20mm × 15mm silver-foiled jet rectangle stone *Article 4610*
- one Swarovski Elements 20mm × 15mm silver-foiled silver shade rectangle stone *Article 4610*
- six 18mm × 13mm rhodium-plated 4-prong settings
- three 20mm × 15mm rhodium-plated four-prong settings
- nine BeadFix™ adhesive squares
- 50" (127cm) 4mm 4-sided vintage tube copper ox-plated bar chain
- two 6mm copper jump rings
- one copper toggle ring
- one copper Greek style clasp

TOOLS

- 80-grit sandpaper
- chain-nose pliers
- Curved Squeeze Scissors
- metal hole punch
- nylon jaw chain-nose pliers
- round-nose pliers
- safety goggles
- tin snips

à la mode
Wear this piece with a classic long black dress—the solid color will intensify the richness of the crystal stones and the glow of the copper. Let the bold pendant rest against the fabric and adjust the chain to your desired length. Copper or old gold metallic shoes will give you a fashion police pass forever!

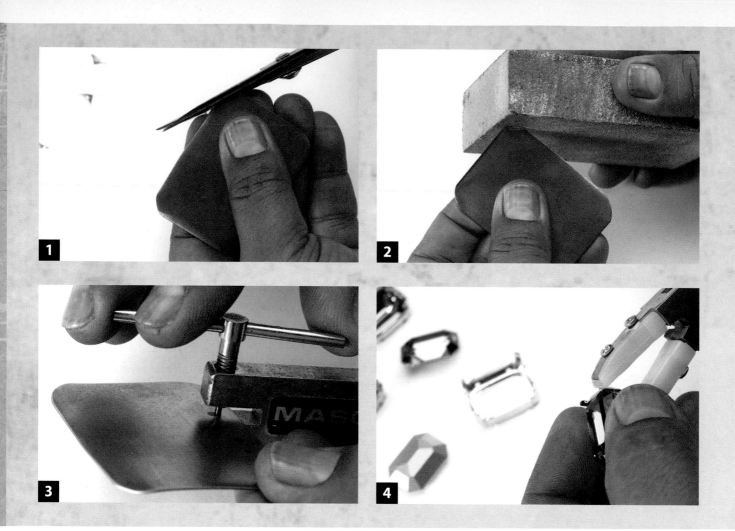

1 Using tin snips, cut copper sheet into 2 pieces, measuring 2" × 2½" (5.1cm × 6.4cm) and 1½" × 2" (3.8cm × 5.1cm). Use the snips to round all the corners.

2 Use sandpaper to file the edges of the copper sheet rectangles to remove any sharpness. Rough the front and back surfaces of each piece with the sandpaper to add texture.

3 Using a metal hole punch, punch a hole at the top left and top right of the 1½" × 2" (3.8cm × 5.1cm) piece of copper sheet. Make sure the holes will accommodate 10mm jump rings freely. Punch 2 more holes near the lower edge of the 1½" × 2" (3.8cm × 5.1cm) piece approximately ⅛" (3mm) from the bottom edge ½" (1.3cm) from each side.

Place the 2" × 2½" (5.1cm × 6.4cm) piece of copper sheet so it is centered horizontally beneath the smaller piece. Punch 2 holes in the larger rectangle, ⅛" (3mm) from the top edge, lining them up with the 2 bottom holes on the smaller rectangle.

4 Set each stone into its mounting (corresponding stones and mountings are listed in the same size). Use nylon jaw pliers to bend in the prongs.

designer tips

• To make sure the holes in the copper sheet rectangles are punched in the right places, mark the holes with a marker before punching them.

• Remember to wear safety goggles when handling the copper sheet. No one likes shards of copper sheet in the eye!

• When bending in the prongs on the stone mountings, use care not to tighten the prongs too much, as the edges of the crystal stones can chip.

5 Peel the protective paper from a BeadFix adhesive square and adhere it to the back of a set stone, pressing firmly. Trim any excess adhesive with squeeze scissors. Repeat this process for all stones.

Apply 3 18mm × 13mm set stones to the smaller copper sheet rectangle, using the image on page 86 as a guide. Apply the remaining set stones to the larger copper sheet rectangle.

6 Connect the copper rectangles with 2 10mm jump rings, using the holes punched in Step 3.

7 Cut 4 pieces of 4-sided copper chain, each measuring 12½" (31.8cm). Attach 2 pieces of chain to a 10mm jump ring and then to the left hole at the top of the smaller copper rectangle. Repeat for the other side of the pendant and the other 2 pieces of chain.

8 Connect the chains from the right side of the necklace to a 6mm copper jump ring. Connect a toggle ring to the jump ring and close it. Connect the chains from the left side of the necklace to a 6mm copper jump ring. Connect a copper Greek clasp to the jump ring and close it.

SOURCES Beadalon, Swarovski

double sunburst

Sometimes an intriguing jewelry component is inspirational in itself. This Art Deco sunburst carried my imagination away. I wanted to exploit its kitschy and glossy surface and retro shape, so I created this asymmetrical design. A chain fashioned from flat disc and marquis-shape spacer beads not only emphasizes the shine of the focal piece, but also adds balance to its volume. It has an old downtown Las Vegas atmosphere, and, just like Vegas, I want you to have fun with it.

MATERIALS

- one silver-color plastic sunburst pendant
- one gold-color plastic sunburst pendant
- one hundred sixty 4mm gold-plated jump rings
- twenty silver-plated 2-hole marquis-shape spacer beads
- sixty-six gold-plated 2-hole flat disc spacer beads
- thirty-four gold-plated 2-hole marquis-shape spacer beads
- thirty-three silver-plated 3-D spacer beads
- one small flower keychain ring
- two 10mm silver-plated jump rings
- two 8mm silver-plated jump rings
- one 6mm gold-plated jump ring
- one extra-large gemstone-tipped toggle bar

TOOLS

- 2-part clear epoxy
- chain-nose pliers
- flat-nose pliers
- jump ring opening/closing tool

à la mode *Minimalism is key in this ultra-modern shoulder-padded black dress. A slice of urban New York mingles with a touch of modern Japanese design, creating the perfect backdrop to show off this asymmetrical necklace. A well-structured hair style takes this look straight to the top, making the jewelry appear more expensive than it really is. Mission accomplished!*

1 Mix equal parts of 2-part clear epoxy, following the manufacturer's instructions. Carefully glue the silver-color and gold-color plastic burst pendants together in a nesting position. Set this component aside and allow it to dry for 24 hours.

2 Open 160 4mm gold-plated jump rings using a jump ring opening/closing tool. Slide the tool onto your right index finger and pick up a jump ring with chain-nose pliers. Hold the right side of the jump ring with the pliers and insert the left side into the slit on the jump ring tool. Twist the chain-nose pliers forward or backward to open the jump ring.

3 Connect components in the following pattern, using opened jump rings from Step 2 in between each: silver-plated marquis-shape spacer + flat disc spacer + gold-plated marquis-shape spacer + flat disc spacer. Repeat this pattern 8 times, then add 1 more silver-plated marquis-shape spacer (33 total components). This is chain A.

Repeat this step, using the same pattern. Repeat the pattern 8 times, and then add a silver-plated marquis-shape spacer, a flat disc spacer and

a gold-plated marquis-shape spacer (35 total components). This is chain B.

4 Connect 3-D spacers and flat disc spacers in an alternating pattern, using opened jump rings from Step 2 in between each. Continue linking until you have 37 spacers connected together, ending with a 3-D spacer. This is chain C.

5 Attach chain A to position A on a 3-D spacer (see diagram on the next page). Attach chain B to position B on the same 3-D spacer. Attach chain C to position C on the 3-D spacer.

6 Connect the other ends of each strand of chains A, B and C to another 3-D spacer in the same positions on the diagram. Attach this 3-D spacer to a flower key ring with an 8mm jump ring.

E

D

A

C

B

8 Thread the opened 10mm jump ring through the hole in the silver-color burst pendant.

9 Use the pattern from Step 3 to connect 20 spacers, but replace all silver-plated marquis-shape spacers with gold-plated ones. Use the pattern from Step 4 to connect 19 spacers. Slide 1 end of each chain onto a 10mm jump ring and then connect the jump ring to the hole in the gold-color burst pendant.

10 Connect the loose ends of the chains from Step 9 to a 6mm jump ring. Connect an 8mm jump ring to an extra-large gemstone-tipped toggle bar, and then to the 6mm jump ring.

7 Use the pattern from Step 3 to connect 7 spacers. Connect this piece to position D on 3-D spacer from Step 5. Use the pattern from Step 4 to connect 8 spacers. Connect this piece to position E the same 3-D spacer. Open a 10mm jump ring and slide it onto position E, but do not close it.

SOURCES Beadalon, Elvee/Rosenberg

carnival parade

This chapter is a celebration of colors and textures that showcase fun and easy-to-make projects. I wanted to create an upbeat mood by mixing gemstones, glass, pearls, acrylic and metal, and along the way I found some unexpected and unique uses for jewelry components. The variety of beads in the market is incredible, and I wanted to bring to this book some popular beads that I don't normally work with.

Clasp On (see page 96) is a versatile design constructed with a variety of clasps, showcasing how components can be used in ways other than their original intent. Fiesta in Wonderland (see page 104) is a piece with a playground-like mood. I mounted flat Lucite triangle pendants

on top of one another and enhanced them with beautiful lampwork beads. I was astounded after my discovery of sponge and acrylic puzzle beads; from these two components I designed *Rock the Haus* (see page 108), an appealing piece that combines sponge and acrylic with papier mâché and crystals for an original idea with an unusual color palette.

In this parade of textures, colors, medias and findings, you'll learn that no matter what technique you work with, it's important to be amused during the process and keep your mind open to experiments. Doing so will help you create pieces that truly express your personality.

clasp on

Sometimes subtle components, such as pearl necklace clasps, are so refined that you're inspired to make them the main event. This necklace is composed primarily of clasps linked with tons of shimmering dichroic glass beads and pendants, resulting in an original fusion of white metal and colorful glass—a definite "think-outside-the-box" design. The assembly is similar to *Extravaganza* (see page 12), a rosary-style linked necklace. It's a wire wrapper's dream!

MATERIALS

- 4' (1.2m) 20-gauge silver plated German style wire
- twenty-two 3mm silver-plated spacer beads
- three 10mm × 10mm silver/blue/black dichroic cube beads
- three 10mm × 10mm pinched cobalt blue dichroic cylinder beads
- two 14mm × 10mm silver/black swirl dichroic tube beads
- one 20mm × 16mm green/blue dichroic twisted flat bead
- two 10mm × 10mm chessboard white dichroic square beads
- six 10mm × 19mm silver-foiled dichroic rectangle charm beads
- three 15.7mm round heavy 1-crystal Upper Clasp™ clasps
- four 16.3mm round brushed Upper Clasp™ clasps
- four 7mm × 14.2mm cross heavy Upper Clasp™ clasps
- eleven 16.3mm × 8.7mm plain duet Upper Clasp™ clasps
- twenty-two 4mm silver jump rings
- eleven 6mm sterling silver jump rings
- three 19mm × 9mm blue dichroic triangle pendants
- two 32mm × 9mm blazing blue dichroic long drop pendants

TOOLS

- chain-nose pliers
- flush cutters
- round-nose pliers

variation *You can downscale your necklace and turn it into a casual link bracelet. Consider a gold palette sprinkled with dichroic and gemstone accents. Wear it during the fall season and watch all your girlfriends get jealous.*

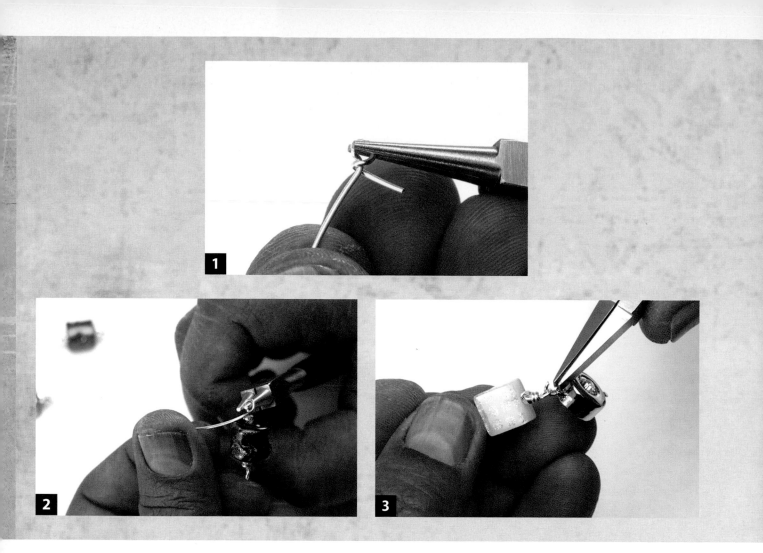

1 Using round-nose pliers, make a wrapped loop at the end of a 4" (10.2cm) piece of German style wire.

2 String on a silver-plated spacer bead, one of the dichroic beads and another spacer bead. Make another wrapped loop at the end of the wire and trim the excess. Repeat this step 21 times until all of the dichroic beads have been made into links.

3 Connect 1 of the Upper Clasps to a dichroic link made in Step 2 by opening a 4mm jump ring and connecting the clasp to the component. Close the jump ring. Continue attaching Upper Clasps to dichroic links in a random pattern, using a 4mm jump ring in between each link.

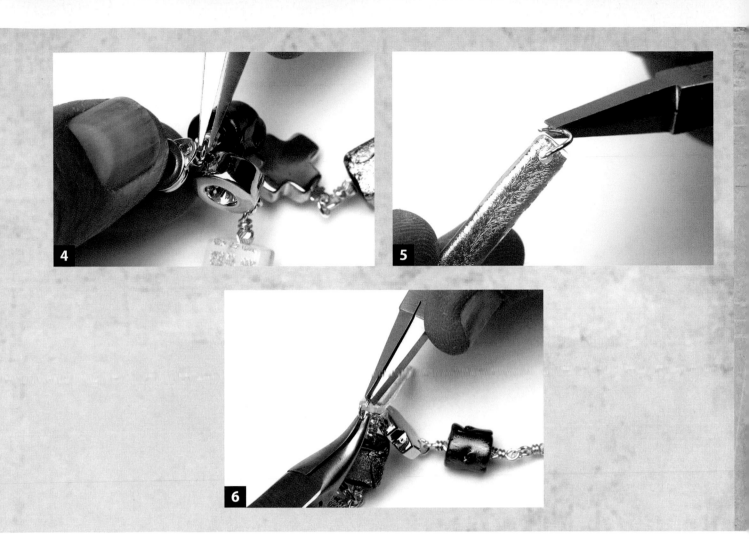

4 Open a 4mm jump ring and thread the side of a duet Upper Clasp between links made in Step 3, skipping every other link.

5 Open 11 6mm jump rings and slide 1 onto each of the dichroic pendants and set aside.

6 Attach 1 of the pendants from Step 5 to 1 of the 4mm jump rings that is connected to the opening side of an Upper Clasp on the necklace. Close the jump ring gently. Repeat Step 6 until all pendants are placed around the necklace.

designer tip

With so many clasps on this necklace, it is extremely easy to shorten the piece or make a couple of bracelets out of it. Some of the Upper Clasp clasps are interchangeable with each other, so it's completely modular and changeable.

SOURCES Beadalon, Paula Radke Dichroics

parquet earrings

This pair of earrings has all the ingredients you'll need to take basic jewelry skills to the next level. I covered half of the bold metal square links with velour rubber tubing for an awe-inspiring effect and combined colors and textures not normally seen together: the subtle sparkle of dichroic glass, the silky surfaces of pearls and the deep tones of amethyst.

MATERIALS

- 4' (1.2m) 24-gauge silver-plated German style wire
- two 7mm x 9mm amethyst faceted teardrop briolettes
- two 7.3mm × 5.9mm dichroic blue/silver tube beads
- four 12/0 gold-lustered hexagon seed beads
- ten 7mm–8mm light gray freshwater baroque pearl beads
- ten 2" (5.1cm) silver-plated head pins
- eight 4mm silver-plated jump rings
- two 7.1mm × 6.3mm dichroic blue/silver cube beads
- four 20mm × 20mm silver-plated square diamond-cut Quick Links™
- 7" (17.8cm) black velour tubing
- two 9mm silver-plated jump rings
- two silver-plated back loop ear wires
- two 6mm silver-plated jump rings

TOOLS

- flush cutters
- chain-nose pliers
- round-nose pliers

variation
A pair of earrings is a good test-driving for an unusual color palette. An exquisite combo was created on this version with chocolate pearls, citrine briolette and glitzy pink beads to cause visual impact. If you like the result, you can redo it on a much larger piece.

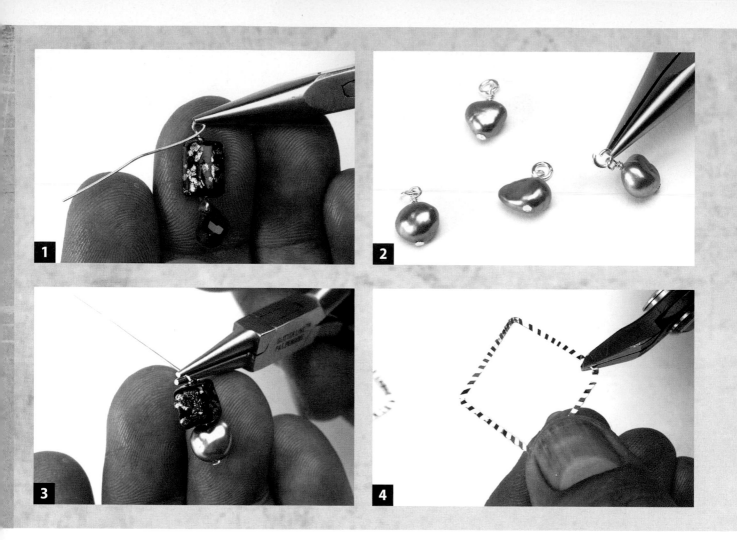

1 Cut a 3" (7.6cm) length of German style wire. Make a drop with this wire and an amethyst briolette. String a dichroic tube and a seed bead onto the wire and make simple loop at the end. Trim the excess wire.

2 Slide a pearl bead onto a head pin, make a wrapped loop and trim the excess wire. Attach a 4mm jump ring to the wrapped loop and close it gently. Repeat this step 3 more times to create 4 pearl drops

3 Slide a pearl bead, a dichroic cube bead and a seed bead onto a head pin. Make a simple loop at the end and trim the excess wire.

4 Using flush cutters, cut 1 of the corners from a Quick Link. Cut about ⅛" (3mm) of metal on each side of the corner to remove the entire corner from the link. Repeat this with a 2nd Quick Link.

5 Cut 4 pieces of velour tubing, each measuring 1¾" (4.5cm). Slide a piece of tubing onto the cut end of a Quick Link piece so that it covers the cut-out corner of the link. Repeat this step with the other cut Quick Link.

6 Open a 9mm jump ring and slide on the following: pearl drop + amethyst/dichroic tube drop + pearl drop + Quick Link (metal side). Before closing the jump ring, slip the 2nd Quick Link (tubing side) into the jump ring. Close the jump ring gently.

7 Open a 6mm jump ring and slide on the following: pearl drop + pearl/dichroic cube drop + pearl drop. Before closing, attach this jump ring to the top Quick Link (metal side).

8 Open a 4mm jump ring and slide on an ear wire. Attach the 4mm jump ring to the 6mm jump ring. Repeat Steps 1–8 to make a 2nd earring.

designer tip

To lend a subtle edginess to your earrings without compromising the overall look, switch out the positions of dichroic cubes and tubes or teardrop briolettes.

SOURCES Beadalon, Rocky Mountain Gems & Minerals

fiesta in wonderland

This color explosion will wow you and everyone who sees it. Delightful lampwork beads in fiesta shades makes this a party on your neck. The colored wire makes a great accent for the brightly colored beads, and the triangular pendant adds a nice touch of asymmetry and unpredictability. Get a piñata and invite your friends over for a party in the fantastic and surreal world of Alice.

~ For Margot Potter.

MATERIALS

- four BeadFix™ adhesive squares

- two 60mm × 40mm yellow acrylic triangle pendants

- one 60mm × 40mm pink acrylic triangle pendant

- three 6mm clear dichroic glass cabochons (1 each of purple, pink and green)

- 18" (45.7cm) each of 20-gauge Artistic Wire™ in brown, pink, cobalt blue, orange and purple

- four 28mm × 14.5mm fancy lampwork barrel beads (1 each of green, yellow, red and blue)

- six 14mm × 7.3m fancy lampwork disc beads (2 of green, 1 each of yellow, orange, red and blue)

- five 13mm fancy lampwork round beads (1 each of green, yellow, orange, red and blue)

- ten 6mm copper jump rings

- one brown leather and metal purse closure

TOOLS

- chain-nose pliers

- flush cutters

- round-nose pliers

- scissors

à la mode *A hip pair of white denim jeans is always welcome when worn with a mellow yellow airy top with some embroidery work around the neckline. The necklace should rest against your skin. Top off the look with a pair of platforms and you're ready to roll!*

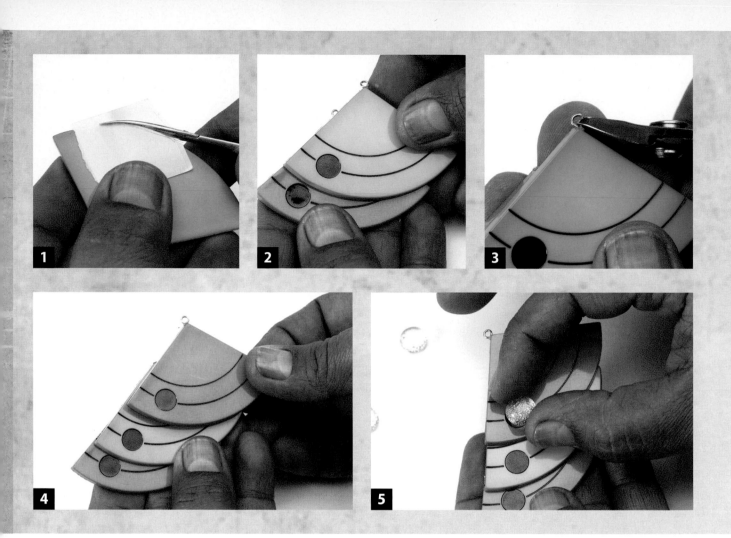

1 Trim 1 edge of a BeadFix adhesive square to follow the curve of the pendant.

2 Peel the paper backing from the adhesive square and adhere it to the top of the front side of a yellow pendant. Press the pink pendant on top of the yellow pendant, positioning them so the yellow pendant peeks out from beneath the pink pendant.

3 Using flush cutters, cut the loops off the tops of the pink pendant and yellow pendant.

4 Adhere a 2nd yellow pendant to the top of the pink pendant using the same method as in Steps 1–2.

5 Trace the shape of a dichroic cabochon onto an adhesive square and cut out the shape. Carefully peel off the paper backing and adhere it to the bottom of the cabochon, pressing firmly. Peel off the other paper backing and adhere the cabochon to a black dot on 1 of the pendants. Repeat this step to add a cabochon to each dot, creating your desired color pattern.

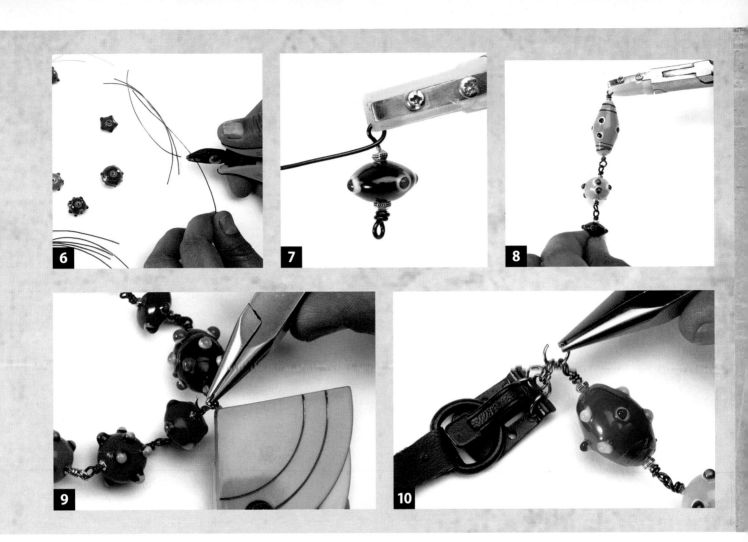

6 Cut 3" (7.6cm) pieces of each color of colored wire in amounts that correspond with the colors and amounts of lampwork beads: brown wire is paired with green beads, pink wire with yellow beads, orange wire with orange and red beads, and purple wire with blue and purple beads.

7 Create a link from a lampwork bead and its corresponding wire color. Make a wrapped loop at the end of the wire, slide on a metal spacer, a lampwork bead and a metal spacer, and then make a half loop, but do not wrap it. Begin making a 2nd link and slide the wrapped loop onto the 1st link. Finish the wrapped loop on the 1st link.

8 Connect links using the following pattern: all purple beads + all blue beads + all red beads + 6mm copper jump ring + all orange beads + all yellow beads + all green beads.

9 Attach the top loop of the triangle pendant to the 6mm copper jump ring at the center of the necklace.

10 Attach a 6mm copper jump ring to the last green bead on the necklace. Attach the leather side of the purse clasp to this jump ring.

Attach a 6mm copper jump ring to the other end of the necklace. Attach a pair of jump rings to this 1st jump ring, then another pair of jump rings to the 1st pair. Attach 1 jump ring to each of the jump rings making up the 2nd pair. Attach these last jump rings to the other half of the purse clasp.

designer tip

The purse clasp adds an unusual but striking feature to this necklace, but feel free to replace it with your favorite clasp.

SOURCES Beadalon, Elvee/Rosenberg

rock the haus

In this design, I fused retro acrylic puzzle beads with a bold '70s aesthetic to make a casual and contemporary yet timeless look. In the early 1900s, the Bauhaus art movement rethought shapes before modernism got going. The legacy of this movement still influences artists from all over the world. In *Rock the Haus*, what is seen at first glance as repetitive and disconnected only accentuates the necklace's texture and depth.

MATERIALS

- two small brown acrylic pumpkin puzzle beads
- two large white acrylic pumpkin puzzle beads
- 25" (63.5cm) 19-strand .018" (0.5mm) red stringing wire
- two silver-plated EZ-Crimp™ ends
- 7" (17.8cm) frosted tubing
- two clear acrylic cone ends
- thirty-six Swarovski Elements 5mm light topaz foiled sew-on stones *Article 3128*
- two Swarovski Elements 5mm smoked topaz round beads *Article 5000*

- two Swarovski Elements 6mm crystal comet argent light round beads *Article 5000*
- two 23mm yellow sponge round beads
- two 24mm silver papier mâché round beads
- two 28mm silver papier mâché round beads
- two 30mm yellow sponge round beads
- one 32mm silver papier mâché round bead
- one silver-plated EZ Lobster™ clasp
- two 7mm silver-plated sparkle crimp covers

TOOLS

- chain-nose pliers
- EZ-Crimp™ Pliers
- flush cutters
- round-nose pliers
- Sbeady™ wire needle

à la mode
A bold necklace can take you to many directions when it comes to style. Here, this girl is on the go. A bold print top with a solid cotton skirt is a great look for shopping on a Saturday morning, especially when paired with flip-flops and an urban beach bag. It's okay to go understated and let the necklace do the talking.

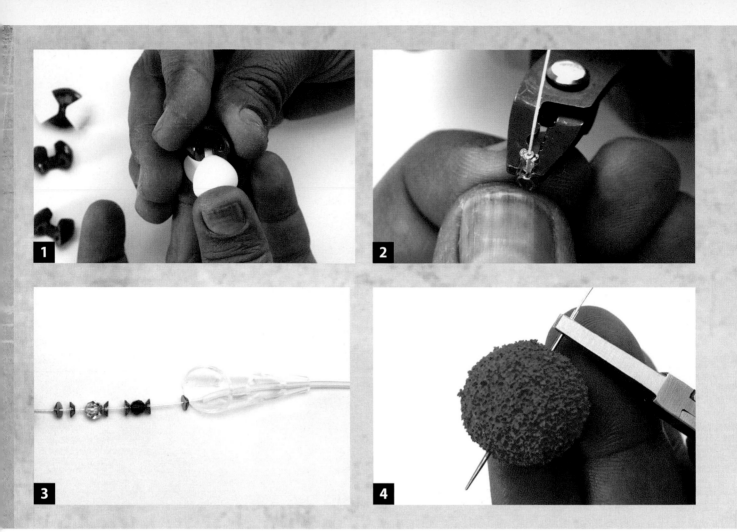

1 Pull apart a brown acrylic bead and a white acrylic bead, leaving 2 C-shaped halves. Slide the smaller brown bead half into the opening in the larger white bead half and push it until it is against the bottom portion of the white bead. Repeat this until you have 4 bicolor puzzle beads.

2 Thread 25" (63.5cm) of stringing wire into an EZ-Crimp End. Use EZ-Crimp Pliers to squeeze the end onto the wire.

3 Cut 2 pieces of frosted tubing, each measuring 3½" (8.9cm). String the following onto the stringing wire: 3½" (8.9cm) piece of tubing + acrylic cone + 2 sew-on stones, back to back + smoked topaz + 2 sew-on stones, back to back + comet argent + 2 sew-on stones, back to back.

4 Thread the stringing wire into a Sbeady wire needle. Hold the needle with chain-nose pliers and thread it through the middle of a 23mm yellow sponge bead. Once you have passed through the bead, take the needle off the stringing wire. (Use this technique whenever stringing a sponge bead.)

5 Continue stringing on components as follows: 2 sew-on stones, back to back + 24mm papier mâché + 2 sew-on stones, back to back + bicolor puzzle bead + 2 sew-on stones, back to back + 28mm papier mâché + 2 sew-on stones, back to back + 30mm yellow sponge + 2 sew-on stones, back to back + bicolor puzzle bead + 2 sew-on stones, back to back + 32mm papier mâché.

6 Repeat the pattern from Steps 3–5 in reverse to finish the other half of necklace, omitting the center 32mm papier mâché bead. Trim the wire, leaving ¼" (6mm) of excess. Thread the wire through an EZ-Crimp End and use EZ-Crimp Pliers to squeeze the end onto the wire.

7 Close a 7mm crimp cover over the rubber tubing about ½" (1.3cm) above the acrylic cone. Repeat on the other end of the necklace.

8 Attach a lobster claw clasp to 1 end of the necklace.

designer tip

This necklace delivers a big look, but it is extremely lightweight due to the mix of acrylic, sponge and papier mâché beads. If you want to add more pizazz, replace a couple of the papier mâché beads with sterling silver beads or 14mm Lucite faceted rondelles.

SOURCES Beadalon, Elvee/Rosenberg, Swarovski

spatial spheres

Years ago, I created wire-caged beads with white stringing wire that mimicked atom molecules, but I never wrote down the instructions. This little creation sat in my drawer for months, and when I took it out again, I couldn't remember the step-by-step process. I still had a vague image of the design in my mind, and I was able to recreate the original concept by threading the stringing wire in and out of pierced beads. To soften its deceivingly heavy look, I added cotton ribbon to the back portion, which created a richer mélange of textures.

~ For Katie Hacker.

MATERIALS

- two 18mm turquoise acrylic round beads
- four 24mm turquoise acrylic round beads
- two 18mm white acrylic round beads
- four 24mm white acrylic round beads
- 10 yds (9.1m) 49-strand .024" (0.6mm) white stringing wire
- twenty-one 4mm silver-plated crimp covers
- twenty-two 6mm silver-plated sparkle crimp covers
- twenty Swarovski Elements 15mm × 7 mm Montana blue modular beads *Article 5150*
- five 20mm beige pierced metal round metal beads
- thirty-seven #3 gunmetal crimp tubes
- two #4 silver-plated crimp tubes
- two silver-plated round Quick Links™
- 10" (25.4cm) light blue ribbon
- 10" (25.4cm) Montana blue ribbon

TOOLS

- chain-nose pliers
- Mighty Crimper Tool
- Semi-Flush Cutters

à la mode *The different shades of blue in this outfit will accentuate your curves and elongate your figure. The top should hit right at the waistline. Pair it with well-fitting blue jeans to favor your legs. The necklace is a splash of style that is favored by the wide-angle neckline. A playful hairstyle completes this look of casual sophistication.*

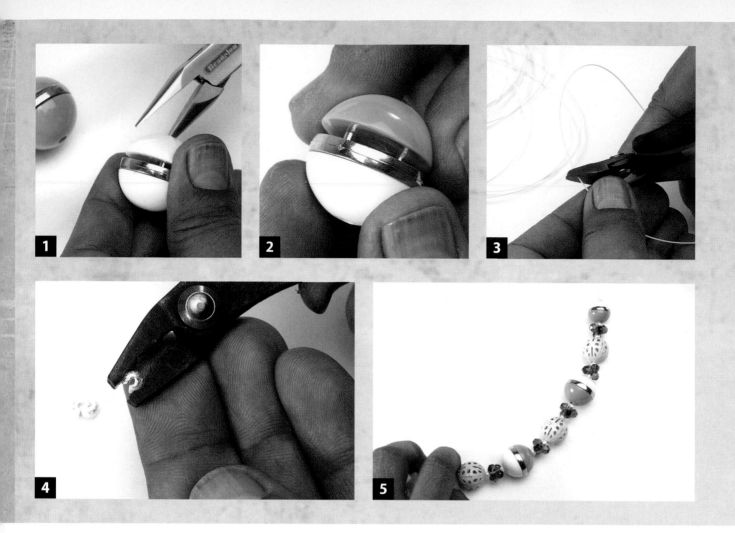

1 Insert 1 jaw of a pair of chain nose pliers into the side of an acrylic round bead. Push into the bead to open it at the seam. Repeat this process for all turquoise and white acrylic round beads.

2 Attach a large turquoise half to a large white half to make a bicolor acrylic round bead. Repeat this process with the remaining large halves and with the small halves.

3 Cut 2 pieces of white stringing wire measuring 20" (50.8cm) each and set them aside. Cut 21 pieces of white stringing wire measuring 7" (17.8cm) each and set them aside.

4 Use the outer jaw of the Mighty Crimper Tool to gently close 21 4mm crimp covers and 22 6mm sparkle crimp covers. Set these aside.

5 String the following onto both 20" (50.8cm) wires: sparkle crimp cover + small bicolor, white side 1st + sparkle crimp cover + 2 modular beads + sparkle crimp cover + pierced metal + sparkle crimp cover + 2 modular beads + sparkle crimp cover + large bicolor, white side 1st + sparkle crimp cover + 2 modular beads + sparkle crimp cover + pierced metal + sparkle crimp cover + 2 modular beads + sparkle crimp cover + large bicolor, turquoise side 1st + sparkle crimp cover + 2 modular beads + sparkle crimp cover + pierced metal.

Repeat this pattern in reverse for the other side of the necklace, omitting the center pierced metal bead. When bicolor beads are strung on, reverse the color that is strung on 1st.

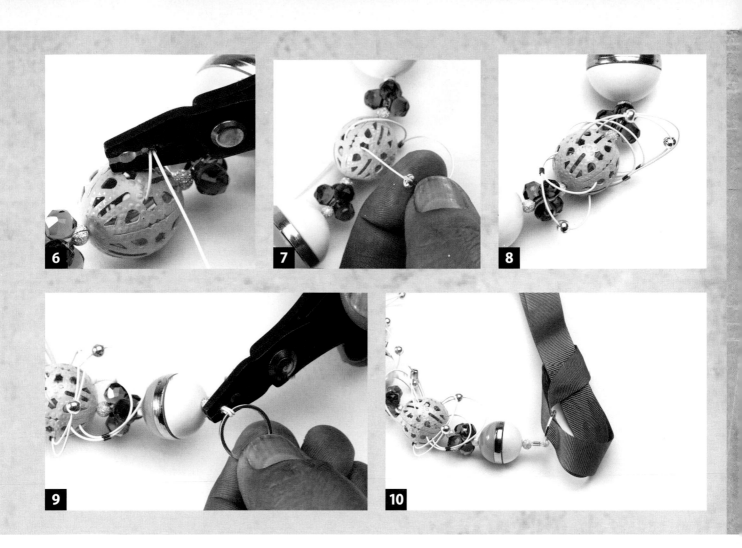

6 Insert a 7" (17.8cm) piece of stringing wire through the center of a pierced metal bead. Bring the wire back around to make a full circle and crimp the 2 wires together with a #3 crimp tube.

7 Thread the longer end of the wire back through another hole in the pierced metal bead. Bring the wire through the bead and back around to make a full circle. Crimp the wires together with a #3 crimp tube. Cover both crimp tubes with silver-plated crimp covers and then trim the excess wire.

Repeat this process to add 4 more double-wire circles to the same pierced metal bead.

designer tip

Before crimping the double wire circles with the crimp tubes, you can adjust the position and size of the circles as desired. Circles do not need to be perfect. Different-sized circles add depth and interest to the piece.

8 Repeat Step 7 with the remaining pierced metal beads.

9 Thread the wires at the end of the necklace through a #4 crimp tube. Slide on a round Quick Link and then thread the wires back through the crimp tube, pulling the Quick Link tightly against the crimp tube. Use the Mighty Crimp Tool to crimp, and then cover the tube with a 6mm crimp cover. Trim any excess wire. Repeat this step on the other side of the necklace.

10 Fold a 10" (25.4cm) piece of light blue ribbon in half. Connect the ribbon onto the Quick Link at the end of the necklace with a half-hitch knot. Repeat this step on the other side of the necklace with a 10" (25.4cm) piece of Montana blue ribbon.

SOURCES Athenian Fashions Warehouse, Beadalon, Swarovski

menswear gallery

As a male jewelry designer, I have naturally created a few pieces for guys over the years. When it comes to men's jewelry, we still have many taboos to shatter, but in this small gallery, I give a nod to some popular men's jewelry classics. You will find bracelets and necklaces on some unexpected combinations: pearls, stainless steel, wood, crystal and cuff links, all the epitome of elegance and trendiness.

< wild sailor
Necklace with sterling silver ball chain, rhodium oval ring and black onyx horn
Length: 19" (48.3cm)

go tiger ∨
Bracelets with red and yellow tiger's eye, wood, blue agate, blue bamboo coral and stainless steel clasps
Length: 8" (20.3cm)

latin lover >
Necklace with lapis lazuli, sterling silver, tablet pearls, a Swarovski triangle stone and a stainless steel pendant
Length: 25" (63.5cm)

casablanca memories >

Necklace with heavy stainless steel chain, various cuff links, stainless steel charms and a black onyx cube
Length: 20" (50.1cm)

steel power

Bracelets with brown and black braided leather and stainless steel clasps
Length: 8" (20.3cm)

shiny dude

Necklace with stainless steel coil, green tourmaline, lapis lazuli faceted cubes and sterling silver sticks
Length: 20" (63.5cm)

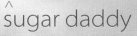

< sugar daddy

Necklace with garnets, black accent and stainless steel chain and clasp.
Length: 20" (63.5cm)

Bracelet with black spinnel faceted cubes, black accent and stainless steel clasp
Length: 8" (20.3cm)

techniques

OPENING AND CLOSING JUMP RINGS

1 Hold a jump ring using 2 pairs of flat-nose pliers.

2 To open, pull the right pliers toward you while holding the left pliers in place.

3 To close, hold the ends with the pliers and move the right pliers back while holding the left pliers in place.

MAKING WRAPPED LOOPS

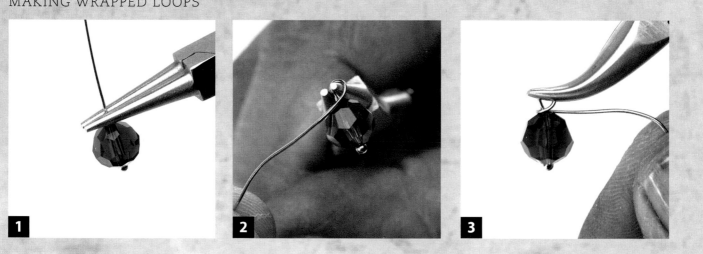

1 String a bead onto a head pin. Grasp the head pin with round-nose pliers just above the bead.

2 Bend the head pin at 90-degree angle using your fingers and turn the round-nose pliers slightly away from you until they touch the bead. Use your finger or another pair of pliers to make a full loop with the wire around tip of the round-nose pliers.

3 Hold the loop with a pair of pliers and use your fingers to wrap the remaining wire around the base of the loop 2 full revolutions. Use a pair of cutters to trim the excess wire, and use chain-nose pliers to tuck the end of the wire into the wrap.

CRIMPING AND USING A WIRE GUARDIAN

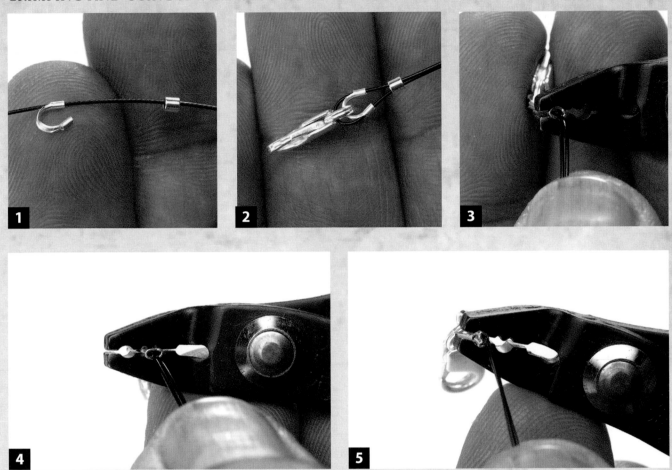

1 Slide a crimp tube and a Wire Guardian onto stringing wire.

2 Thread the wire through the Wire Guardian. Slide a clasp onto the wire so it rests in the U shape of the Wire Guardian. Run the wire back through the crimp tube.

3 Place the crimp tube in the outer jaw of crimping pliers, making sure the wires are side by side, not crossed. Clamp the pliers down to shape the tube into an oval.

4 Place the crimp tube into the inner jaw of the pliers and clamp down firmly to form an indention.

5 Move the crimp tube back to the outer jaw and clamp down again until the crimp tube is nicely folded.

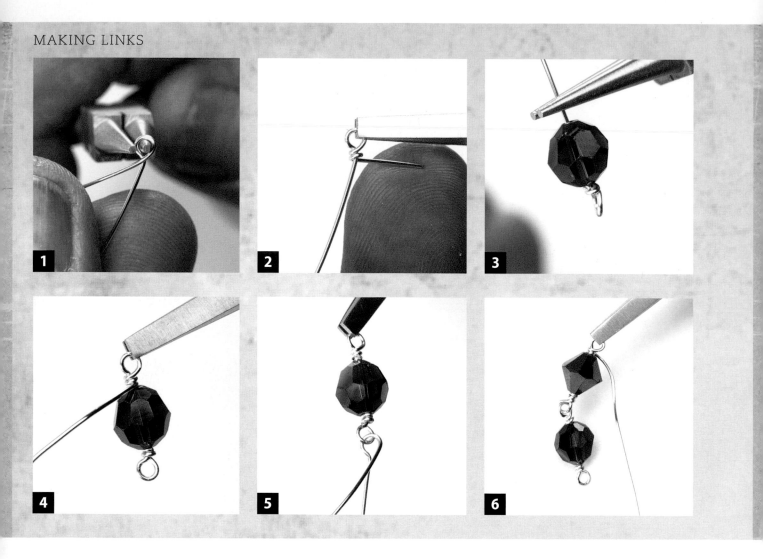

1 Using round-nose pliers, bend the end of a 3" (7.6cm) length of wire at a 90-degree angle. Roll your hand away from you, grab the tip of wire with your nondominant hand and pull it around the tip of the pliers to make a loop.

2 Hold the loop with flat- or chain-nose pliers and wrap the tail around the base of the loop twice. Trim the excess wire.

3 String a bead onto the wire. Grasp the wire above the bead with the round-nose pliers .

4 Make a 2nd loop above the bead. Use your fingers to pull the wire tight as you wrap around the loop base twice. Trim the excess wire.

5 To connect another link to the 1st link, make a loop at the end of a new piece of wire and, before wrapping it, slide it onto 1 of the loops on the 1st link.

6 Wrap the wire tail of the new loop around the base of the loop 2 full revolutions and then trim the excess wire. Slide a bead onto the new wire and finish it by making a similar loop at the opposite end. Continue adding links as called for in the design pattern.

MAKING DROPS

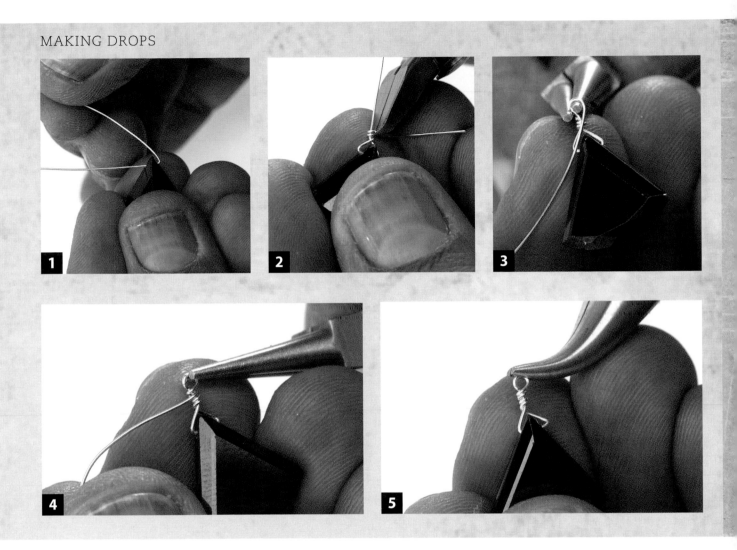

1 Cut a 4" (10.2cm) length of wire and bend the end at a 45-degree angle with flat-nose pliers about ⅓ of the way down the length. String a drop or briolette onto the longer end of the wire, letting it rest on the bend.

2 Use chain- or flat-nose pliers to bend the short wire up and across the long wire. Wrap the short wire around the long wire 2 complete revolutions. Cut the short wire with flush cutters (with the flush side toward the coil).

3 Grasp the longer wire with round-nose pliers. Make a loop above the wrapped wires, using 1 of the tips on the round-nose pliers.

4 Hold the loop with chain-nose pliers and wrap the wire around the base of the loop until the wire meets the wraps from Step 2.

5 Adjust the loop with bent chain-nose pliers so the gemstone drop hangs correctly.

designer tip

The wire lengths used in these techniques are strictly general lengths. If your design dictates a different length wire, follow that instruction for the best results.

GLUING WITH BEADFIX ADHESIVE SQUARES

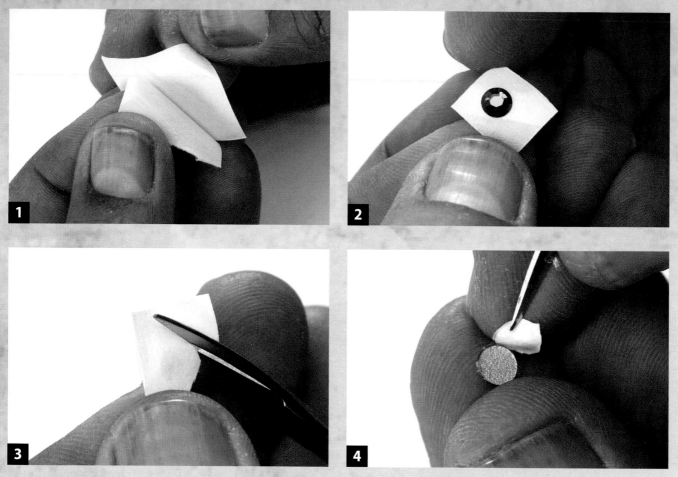

1 Peel back 1 paper backing from a BeadFix adhesive square.

2 Press the stone to be attached onto the exposed adhesive.

3 Use small scissors to cut the excess adhesive from around the stone.

4 Use a straight pin to remove the other paper backing from the adhesive. Press the stone firmly onto a surface as directed by the design pattern.

OPENING PRE-OPENED CRIMP COVERS

Use an opener tool to open a seamless round bead or to enlarge the opening seam of a pre-opened crimp cover.

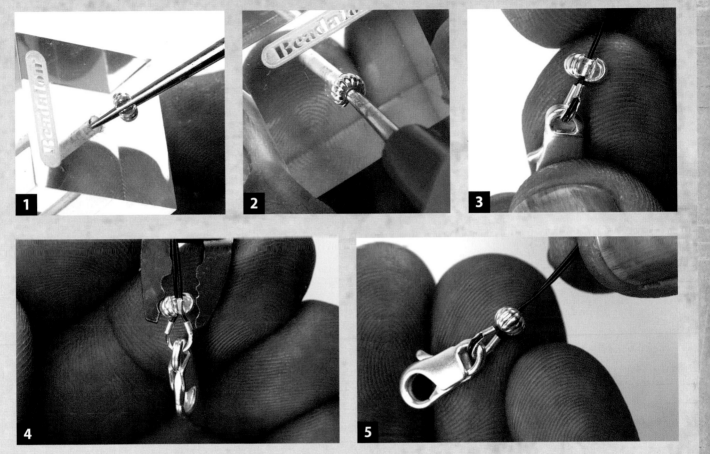

1 Set a seamed bead onto the tip of an awl. Insert the tip of the awl into the hole in an acrylic block.

2 Push the awl into the hole in the acrylic block, forcing the seamed bead open to the desired amount.

3 Place the opened bead over the crimp.

4 Use a Mighty Crimper Tool to carefully close the opened bead.

5 The bead should completely conceal the crimped tube.

KNOTTING WITH A KNOTTER TOOL

When stringing a pearl necklace, for a professional look you should always place knots in between pearls. I knotted the black onyx beads in the *Night and Day Duet* (see page 24). Knots can be placed between gemstones and crystals as well.

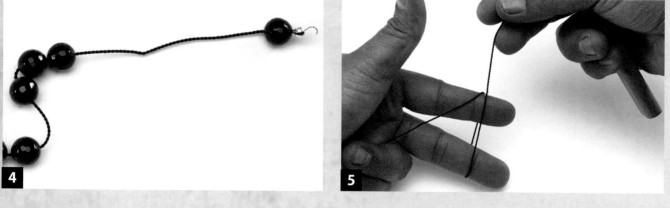

1 Make a double knot in the end of a piece of silk cord.

2 String on a clamshell bead tip and slide it to the end of the cord.

3 Apply a small amount of bead stringing glue to the double knot. Close the clamshell so that the glued knot is hidden inside.

4 String on all beads as directed in the design pattern. Slide the 1st bead up against the clamshell bead tip.

5 With the knotter tool in your right hand, and the end of the silk in your right hand, wrap the end of the silk around the index and middle finger of your left hand.

designer tip

If you are having trouble with the knotter, visit the Beadalon channel on YouTube and search for "knotter tool instructions."

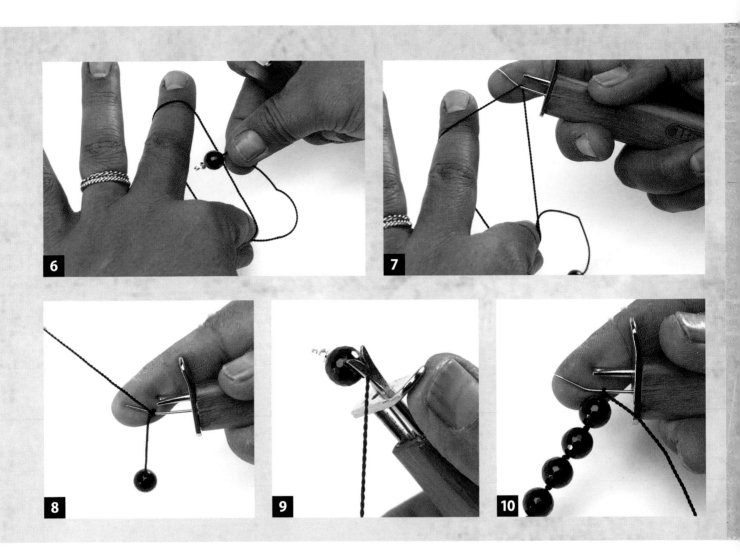

6 Twist your left hand clockwise and insert the end of the strand, with the 1st bead, through the loop on your index and middle fingers. Pull the end completely through, but maintain the loop.

7 Insert the bent-awl of the knotter tool into the loop. Place your right index finger against the awl to keep the silk from slipping off as you tighten the knot.

8 Remove your index and middle fingers from the loop and pull the silk straight up until the loop is tightly around the bent-awl. Continue to pull until there is no longer any slack in the silk.

9 Place the silk into the V portion of the knotter tool and pull it tight. While pulling the silk with your left hand to keep the knot tight, push up on the knotter tool with your right thumb until the bead and newly formed knot are pushed up and off the bent-awl.

10 The knot should be snug against the bead. Repeat the process until all beads are tightly knotted.

resources

Most of the products used to create the designs in this book can be found at your local bead or arts and crafts store. The ever-changing nature of the beading market may make it difficult to find exactly the same beads that were used on particular designs, but similar beads can always be substituted.

Some of the companies listed below have generously provided products for this book.

Athenian Fashions Warehouse
(213) 489-2237
info@athenianfashions.com
General findings, chain and beads

Great Craft Works
(610) 431-9790
www.greatcraftworks.com
Sterling silver clasps and gemstones

Rio Grande
(800) 545-6566
www.riogrande.com
Jewelry supplies and tools

Beadalon
(610) 466-6000
www.beadalon.com
Stringing wire, components and tools

John Bead Corporation
(888) 755-9055
www.johnbead.com
Jewelry and craft supplies

Star's Clasps
(800) 207-2805
www.starsclasps.com
Exclusive sterling silver components

Elvee/Rosenberg Inc.
(212) 575-0767
www.elveerosenberg.com
European components and Lucite beads

Murano Glass Beads
(408) 245-5900
www.muranoglassbeads.com
Venetian, fused and hand-blown glass beads

Swarovski North America
www.create-your-style.com
Crystal components, design tools and a DIY online community

For a complete resource list of each project, please visit: **www.dasilvajewelry.com/modernexpressions**

index

strut your stuff with more fabulous jewelry designs from North Light Books

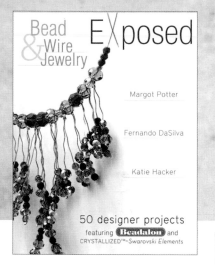

BEAD AND WIRE JEWELRY EXPOSED

50 Designer Projects Featuring Beadalon and Swarovski

Margot Potter, Katie Hacker and Fernando Dasilva

Bead & Wire Jewelry Exposed features over 50 high-fashion jewelry pieces made using techniques that reveal typically hidden components. Beading wire, cording, findings, tubing and chain take center stage in these clever and innovative designs. Each of the three authors, Margot Potter, Katie Hacker and Fernando Dasilva, puts his or her spin on the exposed-element designs, so there's something for everyone.

ISBN-10: 1-60061-159-1
ISBN-13: 978-1-60061-159-9
paperback, 144 pages, Z2508

BEAD CHIC

36 Stylish Jewelry Projects and Inspired Variations

Margot Potter

Bead Chic will show you how to take inspiration that you love and forge your own creative path. After learning basic jewelry techniques, you'll be launched into 36 gorgeous projects. Each project comes with a variation, so you'll learn how easy it is to adapt virtually any project to suit your individual style, making you your own designer. You'll get to play with beads, a variety of stringing materials—from coated wire, to shapeable wire to commercial chain—and findings, all easily found at local and online craft retailers.

ISBN-10: 1-4403-0315-0
ISBN-13: 978-1-4403-0315-9
paperback, 128 pages, Z6942

WIRED BEAUTIFUL

30+ Jewelry Projects to Hammer, Coil, Spiral and Twist

Heidi Boyd

Wired Beautiful features 30+ projects that will get you excited about the many ways you can use wire in your jewelry projects. Best-selling author Heidi Boyd takes you through the ins and outs of working with wire for your jewelry designs. You'll learn how to make wire do your bidding in four detailed chapters: Spiraled & Coiled, Linked & Hammered, Wrapped & Bundled and Knotted & Stitched. Each project includes clear step-by-step photos and detailed instructions.

ISBN-10: 1-4403-0310-X
ISBN-13: 978-1-4403-0310-4
paperback, 128 pages, Z6886

These and other fine North Light titles are available at your local craft retailer, bookstore or online supplier, or visit our website at www.mycraftivitystore.com.